Through THE Valley

Dan Baskill

*A Remarkable Story of a Young Girl's Journey
with Pulmonary Hypertension*

tellwell

Tellwell Talent
www.tellwell.ca

ISBN
978-1-77302-013-6 (Paperback)
978-1-77302-014-3 (eBook)

Table of Contents

Foreword

THANK YOU FOR PICKING UP THIS BOOK, AND FOR TAKING the time to read our story. I had never attempted to write a book before, although many would disagree judging by some of the lengthy emails I've written over time. This story has lain firmly on my heart for some time. During these better days for my daughter, I've decided now is my chance to put our story into words before we lose the notes, emails, and FB posts. Already my efforts have caused me hours upon hours of reliving certain events, correcting text, and redoing paragraphs time and again … and I conclude that a writer's task is no easier than the most difficult jobs I've done over my career in construction. Who would have thunk it!

The title of this book *Through the Valley* doesn't seem so glamorous on paper, yet it rings with a theme I believe most of us can relate to. A Bible verse many are familiar with is Psalm 23:4, which says, "⁴ Even though I walk through the darkest valley,[a] I will fear no evil, for you are with me; your rod and your staff, they comfort me." This passage has several key points which I have come to relate to: First of all, there will be valleys. Secondly, the images of a rod and staff tell me that I will need guidance and even discipline while there. And finally, I don't have to be afraid, for our God promises to walk with me. I take liberal license with this analogy, weaving our family's journey as if on a path from lofty grandeur to despairing depths, and back up. I sincerely hope you can identify with the comparison, for I believe all of us will endure such journeys at one point or another.

I say this with certainty: we will all hit a wall, fall over a cliff (hopefully not literally), and have our staid and comfortable lives torn asunder by an event beyond our control. Human nature causes us to strive to live in that comfortable spot where we are 'in control' and at peace with those around us and the circumstances in which we live. And we get pretty good at being comfortable. We may not live the dreams we had planned for as idyllic teens, but as we settle into adulthood, we find ways of wearing our surroundings like a warm jacket on a cool fall day. Some people are not so fortunate, being born into circumstances far more difficult that most of us can imagine, but for the most part, we tend to live predictable and safe lives here in North America. And then the unthinkable happens. One day we are strolling along a flower-strewn meadow, admiring the views around us, and suddenly, we inadvertently stray off the path, trip in a hole, and are left lying on the ground wondering what hit us and where that terrible pain is coming from.

It happens unexpectedly. It could arrive in the form of a phone call that brings catastrophic news, a consult with a doctor who utters the inconceivable, the slam of a door as your spouse swears they're leaving for the last time… whatever. And we are left hanging on the edge of a precipice with a dizzying view of the drop below; any vestiges of control we once had are now shredded and blown away from our grasping hands. What do we do now? How are we to survive, especially when this shift affects others we hold dear to us? Can we ever regain control and find that peace we all so desperately long for - even if we can't get back to the same place we once were?

I contend we can find peace again, even in the midst of our loss of control. We don't need to wait it out, hoping that one day we'll arrive on the other side to experience peace. In the midst of our deepest valleys, there is a way through, and despite all the fears, pain, and suffering that can accompany the journey, we don't have to live defeated and hopeless.

Interestingly, it is easier the second and third times we drop over the edge, after we've successfully come through the first fall and have lived to tell the tale. Experience is a proven teacher, and can be shared to help others gain perspective in winning their battles. Our journey has given us insight (and I'd like to think credibility) that may be useful to help others navigate their way. I write this not to get a pat on the back for our family, nor to garner sympathy for what you will read, but rather to share a journey that has all the turns and twists of a thriller, the heartbreak of a love story, and some of the resources of a medical diary. It's impossible for me to keep our family's faith out of the storytelling, so I ask for your consideration if you don't see things quite the same as we do.

Bonnie and I make no apology for believing in Jesus as the son of God who died for us and rose again - proving once and for all that He is the way, the truth, and the light. This earthly place is not home; Heaven is, but until then, our God chooses to enter into our lives and circumstances out of His great love. We simply cannot imagine surviving what we have endured without our faith, and we believe that God is trustworthy no matter how difficult and (dare I say it) wrong our circumstances may be. Several Bible verses have been our strength throughout this journey that I shall reserve until the end to share. They will make more sense then. Besides, I didn't write this to 'preach' our beliefs down anyone's throat. Whether you are a person of faith or not, there is much within our journey that can be useful when you trip over the edge - you can endure and overcome the pull of the valley. Please, bear with me!

That being said, we've seen incredible sights and been a part of some truly astounding experiences to not look beyond these moments and see the hand of a sovereign creator. And in seeking our journey's purpose, we have come to believe that the journey is in fact the purpose. In truth, I can't say I believed this at the outset, but as I look back from the perspective of hindsight, I do now: The journey *is* the purpose.

This writing is not mine alone; it is a collaboration of both my wife's and my experiences with our daughter, sprinkled here and there with insights of others who have made our journey possible. Our intention is threefold: First ... we endured (as we still are enduring) and remain intact as a family and married couple. You can too! Secondly, the secret to endurance is to have purpose, and to willingly submit to things beyond your control that are better left in the hands of God. And finally, we've learned somewhat how to navigate the Canadian Health Care system for a best outcome that may prove helpful to others as they walk their own difficult paths. The goal here is to win as a family, no matter the outcome, by maintaining perspective in the midst of a dark valley - a perspective which has been gained in part by leaning on others who have walked there before. Join with me as I turn back the hands of time to set the stage.

1

The Valley's Foreshadow

IT WAS EARLY MORNING, ABOUT TWO A.M., WHEN THE CALL came through the nursery monitor and across the cobwebs of our slumber. We stumbled out of bed, reaching for our housecoats before bolting out the door and across the hall. Hannah's nurse was attempting to start the high-flow oxygen through a mask while looking at us with concern in her eyes. It was all hands on deck as we broke into a familiar routine. First, oxygen - while another felt for a pulse and verified the trace on the heart monitor. As Hannah began to scream and arch, Bonnie pleaded first with Hannah and then with God to stop the crisis from deepening. I began massaging her chest directly above her heart, feeling the pounding beneath my hands increasing rapidly. Then as quickly as I had it, it was gone, and Hannah fell limp into the bed. With no heartbeat present, the alarm changed from a piercing beep, telling us her heart was racing way over the limit, to a continuous tone confirming what we already knew: Hannah was in full cardiac arrest.

Gathering my daughter up in my arms, I placed her upon the laminate floor with a garment under her head before beginning CPR. She had soiled herself completely and her lips had now turned a deep shade of blue, while the hue of her skin had faded to a lighter shade of grey/blue. With Bonnie pleading for her life and the nurse frantically searching for a pulse, I began to compress her chest one-third of the way for maximum effect without breaking her ribs. As I fell into a rhythm, I remember desperately wondering how many more times any of us - let alone my poor girl - could survive this.

It was in late 2009 when we began to notice little things going on in Hannah, our youngest daughter, that seemed unusual. She was five years old, blonde, petite, and of all our children: incredibly sweet in nature. As the youngest in our family, she enjoyed the affection of her older siblings and was the continual delight of her busy parents and everyone who knew her. Hannah was never energetic from birth; she was slow to achieve milestones such as walking and talking, and even at five years of age, she had a nap each day. That was just Hannah, and we were content to let her move along at her own pace.

I will never forget the first time I really noticed Hannah's enlarged chest and felt her pounding heart with my hand. It was during our Christmas break when this first phenomenon caught my eye. In fact, I could see her heart beating strongly from across the room through her blouse, and I recall asking Bon what she thought. In as much as I noticed it then, we chose not to be overly concerned, thinking it was just a part of how she was developing.

As winter turned to an early spring, we watched Hannah having trouble even walking up a slight incline, and without really thinking about it, we began carrying her up and down inclines and stairs to speed up her movements. I remember both Bonnie and I starting to pay closer attention after seeing her have trouble stepping onto our docks along the beach when out for a walk. The clincher came in early spring when we received a call from the school office one day. Hannah's kindergarten teacher had asked that we be notified of a strange occurrence: apparently she had lain down in the field during recess to "rest her heart". Talking with her teacher later that day, we discovered that this had happened a couple of times before, and we were now sufficiently concerned to meet with our family doctor. His diagnosis was calming, that maybe the cause was viral in nature, and to give her time to overcome and heal. Despite the assurance of nothing amiss, we had a niggling feeling that more was underfoot.

Unbeknownst to us, we were approaching the biggest valley of our lives, not realizing it had now begun its siren call to us. How were we to know, and even if we had clued in, what would we have done differently? It's not like we had any previous experience to know what to look for... or did we? Allow me to step back in time, to briefly introduce our family, and to present a picture that in hindsight may have prepared us for the fall.

2

Life in the Foothills

IN THAT I HAVE ALWAYS LIVED EITHER IN THE SHADOW OF the Rocky Mountains, or in their midst, I've chosen to paint our story in the context of a mountainous setting. I was never happier as a young lad than when out in the foothills west of Calgary where I grew up. So much that was memorable to me as a child occurred when I fished, hunted, hiked, and camped upon their flanks, so it is only fitting to place our happy years as a young family in that figurative place. My wife too was born and raised in the mountains east of Vernon, BC on a small rural farm; her memories there are as strong and wonderful as mine. Where our story occurs, we are further west of the Rockies, living in the more verdant hills surrounding the Shuswap. We have passed our love of the mountains on to a new generation - our kids. Therefore, I equate those earlier years to living well in our favourite place.

Together with my lovely wife Bonnie, we have six wonderful children (four of whom are married), ten grandchildren who we think the world of, and a home and business along the shores of the beautiful Shuswap Lake in central British Columbia. Our first four children were born when we were young: two girls, then two boys, who are quite close in age. Meet our oldest, Jessica, then Rebecca, followed by our first son Joshua, and then by John. Seven years after our fourth, we had a shock with the entry of number five - a son, Tim. And then, five years later as we entered our early 40s, we had an after-shock! Enter our last child, a beautiful dainty girl who has altered our world so drastically. This is Hannah, who arrived amidst concerns that Bonnie would experience possible difficulty due to her allergic reaction to Tim while in her womb. To clarify, Bon had developed a relatively harmless but inconvenient illness similar to hives, call PUPPP Syndrome. It usually only affects women who carry male children, and strikes one in every 200 pregnancies. It is rare for a mother to contract it after other pregnancies, so I actually think Bonnie planned it. She could hardly lift a finger for months without aggravating the rash, and left all the household work to yours truly. Nice! Fortunately for me, the sixth time was a charm, and Bonnie could not point to a rash, smile, and direct me to the dish water.

Life was good. Not to say we didn't have any challenges and scares along the way; we did, and we thrived. And we have memories that are priceless to us. Bonnie and I met in Calgary, Alberta, were married, and lived our first ten years there together. In 1995, we made the move to Kelowna for a new business opportunity, and have been British Columbians ever since. For all those delightful years leading towards this story, we enjoyed a 'perfect' family, healthy children, good friends, church, work, holidays, etcetera.

I remember how sorry I felt for myself when we confirmed Bon's last pregnancy, and how devastated we were as we listened to the sympathetic tsk tsks of friends around us who no doubt secretly thanked God it wasn't them who were pregnant at our age. It was our older daughter Rebecca who whacked some sense into us with her reminder that all life is a gift from God: Poor us, being chosen for another blessing, when we could so easily have missed it. So, our perspective changed, and we embraced our youngest girl with a love that is really a testament to the Lord who first loved us. Now maxing our mini-van's seating capacity, our family flourished around our latest addition, and we marveled at how our oldest children were prepped for their own futures as moms and dads because of the whole family's need to care for a newborn. We later captured a cute photo of Hannah in curls, as a reminder of how irresistible she was to all of us. And to think we were so upset at first! Shameful.

As stated, we had a neat and packaged life. It's not that we were entirely blind to what we now see as the real world around us - it's that we weren't impacted with the struggles other families might have experienced as a norm. We had healthy children, jobs, a comfortable home, and hope for the future. Yes, there were some tough losses in our wider family, but not ones that were so close to home that they affected us in a damaging way. I personally felt I could control pretty much anything that came at us. It must sound cocky to you, but my experience in life helped condition me to believe this. Marriage failures occurred to others, problem kids did not live at our house, only old people got cancer, and car accidents happened to bad drivers. As a family, we were at ease with virtually anyone we came in contact with. It didn't matter which race, culture, faith, socio-economic status, or age of the person; we accepted them all and could get along with a minimal effort. My focus was on my family, our plans and dreams, business, and of course fishing (what Alberta boy doesn't love fishing?). We loved the church, sang as a family, visited nursing homes, home-schooled our children, and ran a nice business that paid the bills and gave me a sense of identity. Bonnie was (and is) an incredible partner and leader in our household who homeschooled our kids, sewed cute dresses and outfits, took the lead in our family sing-alongs, managed our business books, and so forth. Lucky me, for meeting her and sharing the life we

have together! And for my part, I was well-liked wherever I contracted, enjoyed our crew of tradesmen, had many good friends, and received an inordinate amount of pats on the back for the amazing family I had. I was living the dream!

In 2004, a family friend invited us to join them camping to the Shuswap, and long story short, Bonnie and I managed to purchase the very campground we stayed at a year later. We did so with close friends, taking it completely over within a year to tackle a major redevelopment. Those were exciting but stressful days as we became totally immersed in public service, political rezoning procedures, and the complex task of physically building our dream resort. There is a story in what we endured in just this project, but suffice it to say the shine quickly wore off, and we would never recommend to anyone to buy and operate a resort! It wasn't what we had expected, took years off our lives, and cost each and every one of our kids something along the way. I'd say for me it was the first real glimpse into a deeper valley where I couldn't control the outcome. Still… we live in a glorious land, and for ten years have been as close as a family can be, with each of our adult kids taking a turn at helping us in the daily grind. And on the far side, we've been privileged to build something that will outlast us, with friends and customers who have all enriched our lives.

It was here, living in one of the finest places in Canada, where we lost our innocence. I don't mean what you are thinking - that was lost long before - I refer to our life in the bubble. Our perfect, manageable world was about to be undone, and we were about to confront the terrifying reality of losing control over much bigger things. For both Bonnie and I, this was foreign territory and one we felt ill-prepared to deal with.

It started with an unexpected challenge at work which quickly spilled over to our family and oldest son.

3

The Valley's Reflection

WE WERE APPROACHING THE EDGE. FROM HERE, I COULD see the shadows blocking out the true depth of an unexpected fissure. We had been living higher up, trading sunset for sunrise over a familiar landscape, and then we'd walked unknowingly towards a strange and foreboding valley. Sometimes loss of control happens in increments; other times it is immediate and unavoidable. Our first glimpse of darker days occurred in an area where I was supremely confident: business.

In that so much of this story revolves around our time in the Shuswap, it is good to understand how the resort influenced our family. We had left a rather typical city environment for a new life in the country, on a piece of land we share with hundreds of others each year. Winters are very quiet, leaving us thirteen acres to ourselves to enjoy while we prepare for the next busy season; summers are out of control, demanding every moment of our time. We are seemingly subject to every whim and demand of the camping public, with our personal family time sacrificed for months on end. Over time we have set some measures in place to help mitigate this strain, and accept that life here is part give and take. We are together as a family most of the time, which is something that so many of our clients cannot imagine. In the energy industry, which employs many of our guests, dads are often away on shift their whole careers, with both parents employed away from the home as the status quo. I imagine many of them envy what we seem to have, and so I do not complain on this front. Where we began to lose control is through a rezoning application we needed to complete. For the first time, I couldn't work my way out of a problem with my hands, but was subject to a fickle public who felt it their place to exert control over us.

The second and in many ways more dramatic instance that helped fracture our sense of well-being occurred with our oldest son about the same time as we started our development steps. As most parents of faith, we long that each of our children see God for themselves and not just as the 'religion' the family follows. Our relationship with God, as Christians, is deeply personal and real, and is one we want each of our kids, family members, and friends to experience for themselves. Bonnie and I might be content to live out our days knowing our relationship is with a real God, but we're open to even more! We've read of a God who was visible to His people throughout the chapters of the Bible, and we have prayed time and again that He would do something remarkable that our kids could see - to show them there was more to their parents' faith than quiet devotion to a system of belief. This is what we love about God: He loves to surprise and answer us in ways we'd never expect. And sometimes, he gives us valleys.

It was the spring of 2006, and our oldest son Joshua was seventeen. He had discovered a new product he felt we could use at the resort for rentals. Actually, he was smitten with the idea, and set out to sell me on it too. We had a ski boat at the time, and some creative crazy had designed a tube that would lift off the water to fly the rider for considerable distances behind the boat. Being quite active and enamoured with flight myself, I did the research and we purchased one from our local boat dealer. We received the tube in mid-May. The water was cold, but our anticipation knew no bounds, so off we went to try it out. We quickly discovered the thing would not 'fly' at the 25mph tow speed listed in the instructions, and in fact had to increase our tow speed to 40mph to achieve lift-off. But as described, this wondrous thing would soar five to ten feet above the wake, staying up as long as the rider could manage the air currents. Joshua was fearless, and we felt the tube would be in hot demand when our summer crowds arrived. Besides, with all the demands placed upon us by the resort, I felt it only fair to do something fun with my son and the rest of the kids who were old enough (and dumb enough) to try out our new toy.

On the May long weekend, our good family friends came up to visit, and as I was too busy with guests, my friend Bevan took Josh out with all the kids to see this tube in action one sunny afternoon. Sometime later (I don't remember when), I received a cell call that Josh had been hurt, and they were on the way back to the dock needing help. I rushed down to find my son in considerable distress at the back of the boat, and knew we had to get him to the Emergency ward in Salmon Arm as fast as we could. Joshua had decided a longer rope was needed to get an even better flight experience. When he was pulled behind the boat, he had suddenly shot up over forty feet in the air. Bevan, seeing what was happening, had slowed the boat, causing the now top-heavy tube to flip over. The forward momentum had driven the tube into a steep descent, and Josh had hit the water on his side doing maybe 70mph. He had retained consciousness, and was able to be dragged over the stern before collapsing. When I met them at our dock, Josh was having great difficulty breathing and could not rise from a prone position. We carried him to our van, and headed off to town without awaiting an ambulance.

Do you know that union policies prohibit hospital staff from lifting a patient from a vehicle to a gurney? When I arrived at the Emergency doors, having pre-warned them we were coming, the staff refused to attend to Josh until an ambulance could be called to assist. My son-in-law Andy was with me. No amount of pleas would move the staff to even look at Josh, and so we waited. And waited. All this time, Josh was getting worse and worse, and we had no idea of the extent of his injuries even though we were sitting only thirty feet from a qualified team of professionals. Bonnie arrived from a weekend ladies' retreat and joined us in entreating the staff to do something. Finally, after my son-in-law threatened to go ballistic and I threatened a lawsuit, they gave us some scissors to cut his wet suit open to relieve the constriction around his ribs. When I did this, I discovered a mass of contusions. I could hear and see his ribs crackling as he laboured to breathe, and I knew he was in critical shape. I ran back inside and finally motivated the staff to send out a nurse. As soon as she saw Josh, she knew he was in trouble, and ran back in to raise the alarm. The ambulance we had awaited arrived exactly at this moment and joined the fracas to get my son inside. Finally! The lesson here is to call the ambulance first if you believe you have a serious matter on your hands - drive-ins should just go to McDonald's if they're looking for faster service!

To make a long story short, an x-ray and ultrasound revealed that Joshua had several broken ribs, a badly bruised heart, and a partially collapsed lung with a hole blown through the side of it from the force of the impact. His lungs were also filled with fluid, and worse, he had fluid surrounding his heart that could over-pressure and stop it from beating properly. They feared internal bleeding. The decision was made to send him by ambulance directly to Kelowna for better treatment options, and we left together to follow the ambulance down from Salmon Arm.

Any semblance of control we had once held onto was immediately dispelled by the crisis at hand. Yet in the midst of this crisis both Bonnie and I chose to take our fears to the Lord, asking Him to intervene and carry us. On our way out of town, we stopped at our church and asked a group of people gathered there to pray for Joshua, and then we hurried to catch up with the ambulance. All the way down to Kelowna, we marveled at how calm we seemed to be after the scare earlier, despite not knowing how he was faring. We call that feeling the peace of God.

By the time we arrived at Kelowna General Hospital and found our son, they had already completed their own x-rays and moved him to ICU. They advised us he could require emergency surgery, and would likely be there for several weeks. We updated our family and the church people who had prayed for us, and eventually went home for a few hours of sleep. When we returned in the morning, we found Joshua sitting up chatting with the nurses. He had already walked to the bathroom without assistance. The resident doctor sat us down and expressed his confusion over what the morning tests had revealed. Josh no longer had broken ribs, the fluid in his lungs had vanished, and even the contusions down his entire side had diminished to almost nothing. He had no explanation, as he himself had compared the x-rays. By noon, Joshua was discharged, and two weeks later on a follow-up visit his body showed no signs of any trauma, including no evidence of the hole that had so graphically been there before. There was not even any scar tissue.

We had witnessed our first off-the-chart miracle to share with our family and friends that would help bolster our own faith in the difficult times yet to come. This was also a brief glimpse into the valley of the unknown, where no one intentionally goes, and no one can understand until they are there. For our part, we were glad to turn away with a great sense of relief. We gathered the family up and returned back to the foothills, rejoicing. We were certain the worst was behind us, and were bolstered by the certainty of good days ahead.

As an aside, we lobbied our boat dealer who had sold us the tube to remove all of the product from their shelves and to demand the same from the manufacturer. We went after the government to halt sales when our local dealer refused, but it was not until an Edmonton lad nearly died, and several others in the U.S. actually perished, that the Federal Government prohibited sales across the nation.

4

Looking into the Valley

THAT WASN'T SO BAD, I RECALL THINKING. THE BUSINESS challenges we could overcome with our winsome personalities and my dogged persistence to problem-solve. My hands were strong, my ambition was at an all-time high, and I felt we could wrest control back from a community who simply needed to get to know us. As for my son Joshua's experience, I thanked God for the victory and confidently tucked his miraculous healing away as a faith-building exercise that we had passed with flying colours. We could share the story unabashedly, perhaps feeling we were now 'authorities' on the subject of miracles. It had happened to us: we had seen our prayers answered; and so what couldn't we overcome?

Proverbs 16:18 states that "pride goes before destruction, a haughty spirit before a fall." I don't think I walked around with a haughty spirit, and I certainly know that my wife didn't, but nonetheless, I had a certain degree of pride in who we were as a family and in what we had achieved. As I write this story now, I struggle with a frozen shoulder that affects my right arm drastically, taking away my ability to work with my hands effectively. Severe nerve pain keeps me awake at night, compounded with the hours I spend each day on this manuscript. But I am determined. And I reflect how the mighty have fallen. This shift from strength of hand to dependence on others to do most of my work aligns perfectly with the lesson of pride I have been learning. I'm not sure how deeply pride figures into the next part of our journey, but I have connected the dots in my own personal walk and I know it does to a degree. I shouldn't be proud of what I can do; my sense of pride must come from what I see God doing. He is worthy, not me. And so, in looking back at the aftermath of our son's accident, we never made it as far out of the valley as we had thought; our return was inevitable, although we didn't know this at the time.

Rewinding further, I need to take you back to the first two years of Hannah's life. Hannah was dainty. Though large enough at time of birth, she was on the low percentile scale for her ensuing baby and toddler years. She would literally choke during nursing, and have milk pour out of her nostrils. She started having ear infections very early when introduced to solid food, which worsened to the point of needing to have tubes put in. However, the tubes didn't solve anything, and Hannah endured cycle after cycle of antibiotics while we waited for her to grow out of her ear infections. She was slow to walk, late to talk, and we had already concluded that her hearing was impaired. Finally, when she was two and only sixteen pounds, our local pediatric specialist referred Hannah to the BC Children's Hospital for further testing. It was in Vancouver that doctors confirmed that Hannah has De George Syndrome, or 22Q Deletion - a condition where a specific gene is missing in the chromosome sequence. Visible evidence of this syndrome might include severe cleft palette, heart defects, and failure to thrive. Although Hannah has none of the usual indications, she does have a lazy uvula, which explains her poor swallowing and the ability of liquids to pass to her Eustachian tubes (connected to her eardrums). There are other effects that might include delayed development, and we have discovered through continued testing that Hannah has been impacted in this way. Under the care of the Cleft Palette clinic, Dr. Loock, and her team of specialists at the BC Children's Hospital, Hannah has made remarkable advances, and we owe a deep debt of gratitude to the many fine people who have committed to helping children like Hannah as their life's purpose.

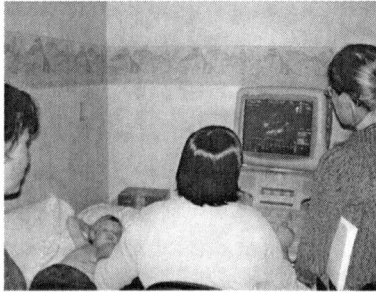

It was on a routinely-scheduled clinic for Hannah's De George Syndrome that we returned to the edge. On April 7th and 8th, 2009 we were able to express our concerns for Hannah's heart to our cleft palette specialist, and to have the focus of the BC Children's Cardiology department brought to bear on her. At first, we were discounted, and it was only through the insistence of Dr. Loock that tests were performed to look deeper. Hannah was scheduled for an ECG, and if necessary - an Echo. When we arrived at the clinic, the ECG lab was busy, so they popped her into the Echo lab to keep us busy. Then it all happened so fast: the test, a consult, and the request to come into the specialist's office for discussion. Dr. Duncan, one of the lead cardiologists at the hospital, had the dubious honour of advising us our girl had a terminal and terrible disease called Primary Pulmonary Hypertension. He stated that had he seen the ECG results first, he wouldn't have called for an Echo, but as a result of the timing, he was able to see conclusive evidence of the disease. We thank the Lord for this small fact. He went on to describe in detail the disease and outcome, and to prepare us for a short life together with our youngest darling. For some of you reading this, you will know the devastation such a prognosis invokes. You may have heard something similar involving the cancer word, or perhaps a tumour. Regardless, there is no comparison to this moment, especially when it is a diagnosis for a young child who, in her youth, has not had a chance at life.

Pulmonary Hypertension (PH) is a relatively uncommon disease that can be caused by other conditions and is more common to adults. Secondary-caused PH can be treated by addressing the initial root cause, so it is classed as a Secondary PH. In very rare instances, no known cause of PH is found, and so it is classified as Primary Pulmonary Arterial Hypertension (sometimes called Idiopathic, or IPAH). The Mayo Clinic describes PH as a type of high blood pressure that affects the arteries in the lungs and the right side of the heart. Tiny pulmonary arteries and capillaries in your lungs become narrowed, blocked, or destroyed, thereby restricting the passage of blood through the lungs to the left side of the heart. Pressure rises in the pulmonary artery and right side of

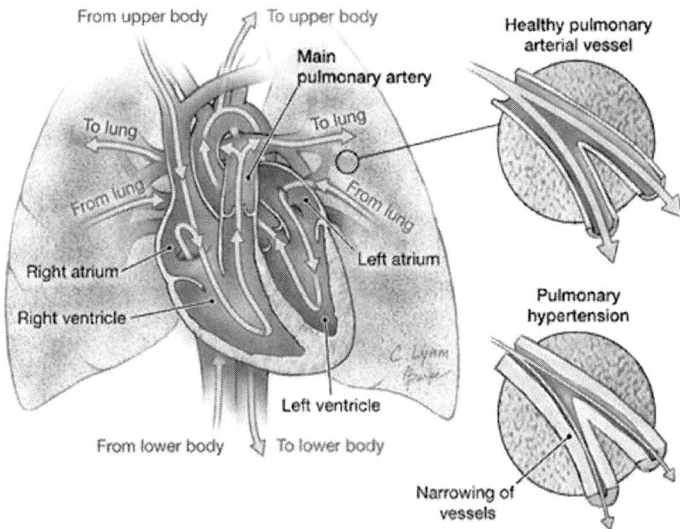

the heart, causing the muscle to work harder to pump the blood through. Eventually, the heart muscle weakens and fails, or it more graphically over-pressures and gives out. PH is diagnosed when the arterial pressures of the right side exceed 25mm Hg at sea level. Healthy individuals have an arterial pressure somewhere around 5-10mm Hg. These pressures are confirmed by a process involving a right side heart catheterization, although a simple non-invasive heart echo can quickly point to the condition.

Hannah's pressures were first recorded at about 70mm Hg, plus or minus a few points. We were told to expect possible side effects to meds, and several PH symptoms common to others who have the disease. These would include back and leg pain, swollen abdomen from fluid retention, 'blue' spells indicating a lack of oxygen in the circulatory system, headaches, and chronic exhaustion. Events would include syncope, or fainting spells caused by a lack of oxygen to her brain. For the specialist in Vancouver, Hannah was his second patient with this disease in his 20 years of practice, and one of less than a handful of children in Western Canada.

We were numb. We had just heard a death sentence pronounced upon our child, and we couldn't take it all in. Later, we dove into the disease, researching all we could to better understand PH, but in those first moments (and days), we were simply... numb. It all seemed so surreal, especially as we began to call our children and parents with the news. We collected ourselves, agreed to a heart catheterization sometime in the next month, and drove back home - both of us lost in our thoughts while Hannah chattered behind us. She was just five-and-a-half years old and innocently unaware. And just like the disorientation of tripping into an unexpected hole alongside a familiar path, we were flung headlong over the precipice overlooking the valley.

5

Falling over the Cliff

THE NEXT COUPLE OF WEEKS WERE DIFFICULT. WITH A FEW words, the specialist had wrested away our control, and our life at home that had seemed so safe and dependable now felt untethered. With the diagnosis to digest, new medical terms to learn and understand, and an uncertain future for our precious girl, we were thrust firmly against the faith underpinnings we had always taken for granted. Our scare with Joshua was as quickly removed as it seemed to have happened, and we still naively thought we could manage the community around us once they saw how 'nice' we really were. Those things we could accept and compartmentalize away as solved or solvable. But we could not do this with Hannah. The fall down was agonizing, for we knew there would be no simple fix unless the Lord were to grant us a second miracle. Don't think we didn't cry out for one! Looking back, neither Bonnie nor I had the feeling we'd escape this one. Hannah was in for the fight of her life, and by extension, so were we. We turned again to our church family, and of course to our own children to join us in our pleas to God for strength and courage. We knew that this was an important step for us. We could not do this on our own, we did not want to, and we knew we did not have to. We had some very good people to lean on, and so we did. At this point, Hannah was unaware of the severity of her situation, and we felt she was not equipped to understand more than simple basics: she had a heart problem that both the doctors and we would work to correct. She accepted this with total trust, and was content to leave it at that.

On April 18th, just a couple of weeks after diagnosis, I was out of town in Kelowna at a spring trade show when Bonnie woke me in the middle of the night in an absolute panic. Hannah had been in bed with her, and our daughter had simply fallen off a cliff. One minute she was there having a seizure, and the next - gone. Bonnie didn't know what to do, other than to pick her up and run to the bathroom to attempt CPR that she had never done before. The bathroom had both decent lighting and an uncarpeted floor, and had therefore been recommended by our trainer. The thump of her limp body on the hard tile was enough to revive her, but Bonnie must have had an agonizing interval before Hannah came back on her own. Sometimes I think of the moments I was not there for Bonnie, Hannah, and my older kids, and I really grieve this. It is a dad's heart to protect his family - to make the bad stuff go away - and I was to learn I couldn't be that guy all the time. I rushed home immediately, leaving my show and booth to my oldest son-in-law and daughter (thank you!), loaded up Hannah and Bonnie, and drove directly to the Vancouver Children's Emergency department later that same day. I believe this was the first time we had left our son Tim behind with Rebecca and her family, which is one of the regrets we have from that first year. Tim was just eleven years old - too young to be away from his parents and Hannah during such a tumultuous time.

Here and there I am going to share some advice to those of you who are - or who will be - forced to navigate the health care world. This is my first comment: When your heart tells you something is really wrong (or your wife who is WAY more in tune with her child knows that something is wrong), then head right to the best source of care. For families with kids, go to the Children's Hospital. Those good folk ushered us right

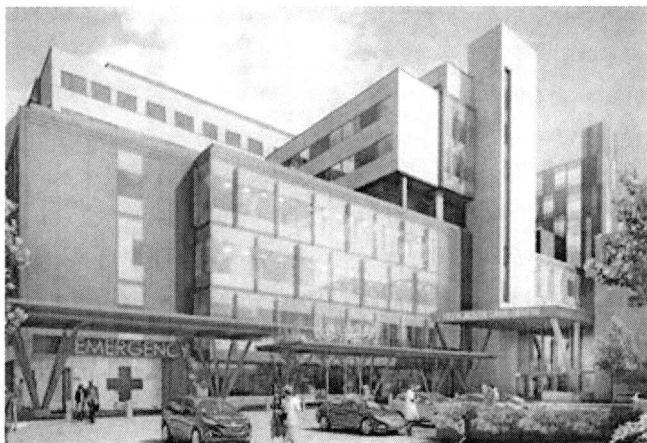

in, and welcomed us into the world of critical care that we would become so familiar with. We couldn't bear the thought of leaving Hannah alone, and so the nurses allowed us to set up a double air mattress right beside Hannah's bed. We appreciated this! In fact, we never left our girl alone in a hospital, aside from a few moments here and there when we walked to get coffee or Chai tea. It's a practice we would continue today, although Hannah is now much older and desirous of her independence, and might alter our habits some.

We spent that first week doing one test after another, watching Hannah's erratic heart on a monitor day and night, while awaiting a heart cath. My parents drove down along with most of our kids and a few good friends to help encourage us. Just before her scheduled procedure, the regular anesthetist came to our bed and basically told me how stupid we were to allow any kind of testing or surgeries as she would just likely die going under. He refused to be the man to do such a fruitless job, and marched off. Bonnie came in and found me white as a sheet, sitting there stunned. We contacted the specialist to make sense of what had just occurred, and within an hour had the chief anesthetist assuring us that this was the best option and not as fearful as advised. He personally undertook the procedure, and we gained some confidence. I think the first guy had his knuckles rapped for violating parent/doctor protocols.

On April 28th, 2009 at eleven a.m., we released our girl into the operating room for her first heart catheter procedure. Bonnie kept pretty good records during this period, and as I re-read the events of that day, all the emotion I felt then wells back up. It's not as bad now, for we have a successful outcome to celebrate, but the terror I felt is still raw in my memory. Never had a valley seemed so deep, or unassailable. Her procedure did not go smoothly, which we did not find out until later, and she had a difficult time through the first two hours of her recovery. During the catheterization, she had been given doses of nitrous oxide, calcium channel blockers, and Sildenafil to view her reactions. At this point Hannah had experienced the start of a cardiac arrest. The doctor was able to fend it off with a shot of Epinephrine. By three p.m., she was gurneyed back to the third floor cardiology ward, and settled in her mother's arms. Her heartbeat was threadbare, but nonetheless steady enough that I walked down to the on-site Starbucks for a much-needed Chai latte (I became addicted to Chais from that point on). Standing in line, I suddenly heard the chime and abrupt announcement that there was a Code Blue on the third floor, followed by a call on my cell phone from Bonnie: Hannah had arrested and was the one in Code Blue.

Now here is a funny thing: It seems that there is a direct correlation with children's hospitals and functioning elevators. When you need them, they're broken. When you don't, they're still broken. That day every elevator was out of commission except for the freight, located somewhere in the back hallways. In my subsequent panic, I didn't even know how to find a set of stairs back to the third floor, and was running around almost aimlessly when our assigned cardiac nurse spotted me on her own scramble up. She led me upstairs, and I ran into a scene straight off the TV medical drama shows. Hannah was surrounded by fifteen or more people. One doctor was on the bed straddling her and doing CPR, another was bagging her, there was no crash cart in sight due to the failed elevators, and my little girl was the colour of her blue hospital gown. I was taken across the hall to a room where Bonnie was, and we fell into each other's arms in anguish. Our well-meaning cardiac nurse began patting Bonnie on her back, advising her to let Hannah go - that it would be better this way - and my woman done reared up and roared! I for one want this woman in my court for the rest of my days, 'cause she will fight like a wounded bear if need be. And really, this was to become our pledge: We would fight for our daughter until we could fight no more, so how dare anyone tell us what we ought to or ought not to do! Needless to say, this would be the last time that particular nurse was involved with our care. We later requested another to replace her; one whom we felt would encourage us to fight for Hannah despite the evidence against her recovery. Incidentally, once the crash cart arrived, it was parked outside Hannah's door with a shot of Epinephrine ready, and the poor young nurse who was first in the room when Hannah crashed was given a week off to recover from her first traumatic event on the ward.

It took the team of doctors and nurses thirty minutes to get her back to a somewhat stable condition. We literally cried out to God, and in the back hall we could hear a Muslim woman crying out to Allah to save our girl. And I swallowed a lot of misconceptions I had about Muslims in that moment, as they are folk just like us who love their kids and will do anything for them. What a sad world we live in with politics and greed ruling the day, when most people just want to live life and dream and hope for their kids. I constantly measure what I read in the news with what I experienced that day and afterwards with many ethnic families we've met in the hospital hallways and rooms. Miraculously, Hannah clawed her way back, but it took almost a half hour for her to stabilize enough to be sent back to the ICU room for closer monitoring.

We felt like a truck loaded with ten tons of bricks had rolled over us, and could only collapse in the ICU waiting room as we awaited permission to enter. A dear friend, Don, happened to be visiting right when all of this was unfolding, and he offered to walk with me down the hall to pray. I remember being quite short with him, telling him in no uncertain words that I couldn't (and wouldn't) pray, but that he could do so for us. Kind friend that he is, he graciously returned to Salmon Arm and continued to pray for us when we simply were not able. He and his dear wife Lorraine have been among our staunchest prayer warriors! I know I was angry in that moment… and took a bit of it out on poor Don. But I didn't stop there: I took a walk by myself to an outdoor patio, and… blew my gasket out to God.

I wouldn't want to write what I said, but looking back, I think it's okay to be honest with Him. And was I ever honest! All my fears, feelings of helplessness, and worse - hopelessness, were on the table in no uncertain terms, and I stormed and raged for some time. I can't say I was suddenly better, or that a blanket of peace descended, or that I even felt heard, but I did leave there spent. More importantly, I really let go. Bonnie and I arrived at this point differently and not at the same time, but we both recall how it felt to give over our daughter to the doctors, to her disease, and to our God. We never once relinquished the right to fight for Hannah, but we no longer thought our hands, our wisdom, or our faith would be sufficient. She was part of a much bigger situation than we could control, and we fully entered the darkest part of the valley willingly. Now, years later, and as I grow in my relationship as a Christian, I want to be less flustered when faced with crisis, and more trusting right up front. Even from a place of helplessness, there will be a way through. If I believe God has all things in His hands, then I should be less tossed about on a stormy sea, right? I know it sounds good when I say it fast, but with all my heart I believe this to be true.

Hannah spent five days in ICU, where we learned that a second crash in twenty-four hours is virtually unrecoverable. Hannah is proof that this is not always the outcome, as we experienced that day and again on several other memorable days in the future. Bonnie called upon her older sister Kathy, a cardiac nurse from Portland, Oregon, to help us make sense of all the medical terms being thrown at us. Kathy immediately dropped everything to drive up for support. We really appreciated this! Back up on the ward, Hannah continued to weaken as the team tried several new meds on her. One of our cardiac specialists thought Hannah might be experiencing reflux that was affecting her vagal nerve, and tried triggering it later that week under full monitoring with chocolate milk, of all things. Hours later, we were trying to get her to respond to us, as her heart rate was plummeting from the nineties down to less than thirty beats per minute. For a half hour I carried her over my shoulder, jostling her to keep her heart beat up over sixty BPM. If I stopped, down it went; when I bounced her around, it rose back up. As you might expect, we avoided chocolate in any form for several years after that! Later studies indicated that frontal lobe seizures were occurring, usually between the hours of two a.m. and four a.m., which no doubt played a great part in her crashes.

Bonnie crawled onto the bed, and after about five minutes of laying perfectly still, Hannah quietly told Mom that "Jesus is here." Bonnie responded in tears, that yes, He was, thinking that maybe the Lord was here to take her away from us. Hannah said, "No… He's right here with me in bed, and he weighs only fifteen pounds! And He hears me!" From the mouths of babes… We believe we've been blessed by God to know His presence, and to know that He has revealed Himself to Hannah in a way she could grasp is truly wonderful. We love this about God.

The days crawled by with more tests and monitoring, and eventually we started a new medicine called Sildenafil. You might know it better as Viagra? Imagine the shock we had when the doctors advised us that this medication was a good thing for her. I had visions of my girl sitting in the back of her class with her arm perpetually raised, or getting an award for the most erect posture (ha ha). It turns out that Viagra was initially created to relax blood vessels in lungs for diseases including Pulmonary Hypertension before a most interesting side effect was noticed during clinical trials. Viagra was consequently pulled out of trials and resubmitted as a recreational product first, before being made available to the medical profession. Go figure! We had our reservations, I can tell you, but of course were willing to trust our specialist who recommended it as the next option. Hannah needed help of some sort.

During her worst times of frailty, even a small change in dosage or the start of a new drug could trigger trouble, so anything new was always introduced under the closest of monitoring. With Sildenafil, she responded well, and has thankfully never experienced serious side effects. Okay, there was one incident where she pointed to a really dark and muscular black man outside a Montana's restaurant when walking with Tim at a later date. She burst out loud that there was a purple man approaching, and no matter how Tim tried to shush her, she kept extolling how purple he was. Tim must have been worried he'd get clobbered! Interestingly, a known side effect of Viagra is for certain colours to be blue-tinted, so perhaps this explains her comments that day?

The BC Children's Hospital takes a team approach to childcare. Each day begins with a gathering of specialists from various disciplines and the primary nurses for a specific patient to discuss the status and treatment options. They gather in each patient's room, sometimes up to ten or twelve people, to review the past day's performance and agree upon the new day's care plan. Usually the parents of the child are present when this meeting occurs, and we never missed a single one. A lot of dialogue occurs, sometimes without tact in front of the family, yet we appreciated the collective skill and care of those meetings. Hannah couldn't hear much of what was said, yet she began to sign small check marks and X's with her hands while looking directly at each team member. We wondered what she was doing, until one day it dawned on us: she was approving or disapproving each attendee for how they affected her. She gave a check for the good ones, and a sharp X for the bad. I pointed this out to the team, and did we ever laugh about that! I imagine that some comments were made once they left, but it really helped engage the person behind the profession for us. Once Hannah was up to dose with no further scares, we were released from hospital care, and were able to return home after a month of living inside the cardiac ward.

With our discharge comes a funny story. We had to be trained to do CPR before we could head out, and a nice gal came down to escort us to the training room. On the way through a corridor, I thanked her for coming to train us, asked her name, and introduced myself as Cathy with my wife Bonnie. We all stopped, I looked puzzled and said that I actually wasn't Cathy, and didn't know why I had said that. The girls laughed their heads off on that one! I attribute my error to stress (grin).

We came away from this experience a bit wiser. We learned we are our child's best defense and caregiver, and we set out to know this disease inside and out. We needed to learn how to help our daughter win. We turned to the internet, where we found a small but engaging group of PH survivors who communicated with each other. We discovered a great resource written for PH families, called "Pulmonary Hypertension: A Patient's Survival Guide" that was extremely helpful. We also were given a couple of names of families with PH that we could call. We chased all leads, left no stone unturned, and became very informed with Hannah's disease as quickly as we could. This is another nugget of advice to all: become your dependent's or your own best specialist.

We had passed our first test of walking down in the valley. Some of the shadows we had noticed from above were not quite as dark and ominous as they had appeared; yet we could not peer far enough into the gloom to see any lasting light. Perhaps we were so immersed in the experience, trying to absorb details to make heads and tails of what we'd been hearing, that we just wouldn't look farther ahead. Our Editor suggests at this point that we possibly 'couldn't', and I like this. If there is no control, no certainty, and hope has been taken away, how does one look ahead constructively? I'm sure we struggled with this as we transitioned through this phase. And really, we had never been there before, so we didn't know what to expect or look for. For some of you reading this, you'll know what we felt from your own experiences. You just live from one moment to the next, hoping and praying for the strength to face the new day, while wondering if the night will ever end. And all the while, we read the Bible, talked together, received quotations and thoughts sent to us by our children and friends, and petitioned God even in our weariness.

6

A First Climb Up

WE HAD GAINED OUR FIRST RESPITE. SURROUNDED BY CHIL-dren in distress, fearful families, and the often tedious days awaiting tests and consults, we had been given the green light to be discharged. Already we had met some very fine people, both within the medical profession and as patients, and our eyes had opened wide to a new reality. The word 'handi-capped' was now part of our family's vocabulary, and the distance from which we viewed other handicapped people in the past was replaced with up front and personal. This bottom dwelling in the valley was a revelation to us.

Finally we were back home. It had been a long month. We were reunited with our son Tim (thanks, Becca), and our middle son, John, who was completing Grade Twelve. We had one hole to repair in our wall, where John had punched the drywall when he'd learned that Hannah had a second arrest that fateful April 28th. He had been left alone with no one to lean on when things went bad, and we regret this still. We were back to our busy development with a looming summer season ahead to prepare for. During our absence, our managers Jocelyn and Martin had lifted a huge share of the burden off of our shoulders, and I managed to provide much of the development's required oversight via phone and email. Getting back into the swing of things wasn't as hard as we had thought it would be, apart from the heightened awareness we now had for Hannah. I recall that our house was cleaned, our yard was mowed, and there was food in the fridge when we drove up. We were surrounded by kind folk!

We could never ever let Hannah out of our sight and reach, so life became a series of juggling time to permit one or the other to do our jobs at the office while caring for Hannah and Tim. Our staff really stepped up to the plate, and a number of fine people from our Salmon Arm church continued to provide meals and support as they could and as needed. By the time our campers and owners arrived, our story was well known to them, and we were given a lot of space and time to look after our girl. We had a lot to be thankful for. On Hannah's first day back to kindergarten after her hospital stay, her classmates rushed to her side and a number of them burst into tears. They each came up, one by one, to hug and greet her, with her teacher Mrs. Sigston marveling at how the class behaved. She later said it was like Hannah had been in the very presence of God, and that a holiness had descended upon the entire room all that day. I had a large rock in my throat, and a raincloud under my eyebrows - some people thought I was crying, of all things. As if! And then I left her in the care of her teacher and teacher's assistant. That in itself was a difficult thing to do, as we were afraid to be out of reach at the best of times. However, it was necessary for all of us to have some semblance of normalcy and routine, and we were learning to commit Hannah to our Lord's care with small steps of faith.

We were beginning to see. We still asked why. Why did our girl have to suffer such a terrible disease? Why couldn't someone just fix it? Why didn't you, God, just heal her? And we still struggled with the future and how we would cope. Our eyes and hearts could now see people around us who were themselves hurt and fearful. We began sharing our struggles honestly, and found ourselves entering into deeper relationships with sometimes virtual strangers as a result. Talking about our hope in the Lord helped ground us in our faith, changing what initially seemed a pointless tragedy into something with meaning. Our circumstance didn't get any easier, but our ability to endure it seemed to.

Hannah gained some strength back the rest of the year, although not without setbacks that took us to the Vancouver Children's Hospital time and time again. We were paying out of pocket for Hannah's meds, into the thousands each month, and so we applied to various government agencies for assistance and relief. As a small self-employed family, we had no medical coverage outside of Medicare, so that entire year was a challenge to make ends meet. We had a mortgage to pay, and hospital trips, meds, equipment, etc. to cover, but we managed. We were in the midst of a public rezone application, and had quite a time accomplishing our normal routines at the park while being singled out by every anti-development group who believed we were fair game. There were many times we felt like abandoning the project, turning in the keys to our bank, and leaving as fast as we could to protect our family and ourselves. But we stuck it out. Our lenders were ever so

patient and kind to us. They continued to give us their trust through this first part of the journey, and for what followed later. They are still with us in financial partnership as we near the conclusion of our drawn-out development steps, and for this we are grateful. We've had opportunity to pray for our account manager, his family, and his boss over the years, which we count as a privilege.

During our trips to Vancouver with some of the new drugs that were tried on Hannah, the drain on our account was such that we turned to the resident hospital social worker for help. We seemed to get nowhere until one day Bonnie kind of lost it in front of the young guy in charge of our case. She didn't stomp her feet or attack him; rather, she just broke down and cried. He was completely shocked, and immediately changed his approach towards her and us. For the first time, we felt he saw us as a family, not a file number, and that's when we started to make headway. He applied on our behalf for medical and nursing coverage without success. At least it was a start. We were still on our own for Hannah's care at home,

and so we settled into our new norm of living ever vigilant, sleeping with one eye open, and hearing even the slightest sounds that would come within the house. Bonnie was able to order a reconditioned hospital monitor that we could use at home in July, after which we lived with a remote screen in our bedroom that we could see at any time. It's still there to this day, but we use it only when she is very ill. Our family doctor also ordered oxygen for Hannah after one PH event in mid-summer - we know that this has been of significant help to her. She has an oxygen generator for nights, and portable bottles that we take whenever we head away from home. Our research has proven oxygen therapy to be an important aide in PH management, and we are thankful for our doctor for supporting Hannah in this way. More advice from us: Insist that your health care workers see you as people. You can help with this by being respectful and honest. Remember, though, they are people too with their own lives and pressures! Threats, poor attitudes, and distrust do little to build a positive outcome.

Hannah was able to return to school again that fall, and her class celebrated each of Hannah's days with incredible kindness and love. I'm not an overly emotional guy, but to watch those boys and girls welcome, include, and guard her gets me every time. Hannah's plight was very real to the school, and all teachers and aides who might be involved with her during the

course of her day were trained to do CPR. We were given special support in the classroom: a dedicated teacher's aide would meet and stay with Hannah on the days she could attend, much to our relief. Our first Education Assistant was a friend named Pat, who became even more important to us as she began to invest in our daughter.

Our home is almost a half hour drive from Salmon Arm, so we would try to have Hannah ride the bus when she was healthy enough so as to experience as normal a life as possible. But it was risky, and finally the school informed us that an unaccompanied bus ride was out of the question. So, we adjusted our routine again to sometimes ride along with Hannah on the bus, or to drive her in for a few hours each day. Either Bonnie or I would stay with her while on the bus or in class, but this was fairly disruptive to our work routines. If Hannah was ill, which happened very frequently, we did some home schooling to try and keep her on some sort of even pace with her peers. We were getting very adept at reading our daughter, and could often head off a more serious health matter by keeping her home.

And so it went; fall moving to winter, and then to spring. At one point during the fall, we made contact with a specialist in Edmonton whom we heard was responsible for most of the research behind Hannah's care. We wanted to hear a second opinion as to her treatment plan. When we first contacted him, he was halfway around the world, yet he took the time between flights to speak personally with us. Impressed we were! We later drove all the way to his clinic in the Edmonton Stollery Children's Hospital, and found a most gracious and caring man who assured us we were on the right path. His name is Dr. Ian Adatia, and we tucked his number away for another day.

With the arrival of warmer weather, Hannah seemed to have more and more troubles as she experienced an increasing frequency of PH symptoms or events including shortness of breath, thready heartbeat, pain in her legs and lower back, headaches, fainting, and so on. On April 6th, 2010, Hannah suffered an arrest at four a.m. which lasted for a few minutes, after which she remained unresponsive for twenty more. She was ambulanced to Salmon Arm, then set up for a flight to the Vancouver Children's Hospital. There, they found her pressures better than expected, so they put Hannah through more tests and consults for the next week to try to identify the trigger. She had a few more bad moments, and talks began about inserting a pacemaker. We were very resistant to this, in part for fear of putting her under, but also for the significance such a device would mean. It was a lot to wrap our minds around. In the end, we agreed to head home and continued to monitor. Later, regular clinics would reveal a climbing right side heart pressure, to which we continued to adjust meds for. Life had become surreal: we'd celebrate anything like it might be the last experience together, while we walked on the edge of suppressed panic over the slightest noise, cough, or look that Hannah would make. For as often as not, it would be a harbinger of the next PH event. We couldn't sleep at nights, often taking turns sitting in her room watching and listening. Hannah attended very few days of school that year, as she was either ill at home, or at home avoiding other children's illnesses. She would sleep a lot, usually until mid-morning, so our schedules were all messed up. In as much as we were at home, we still felt like we were in the valley often, and had no control whatsoever. But we prevailed.

We worked our business, tried to have a semblance of normalcy with Tim and our grown children, and held onto each other and our faith as our only lifeline. Our adult children, my parents (Bon's dad had already passed away and her mom was in a care facility), our closest friends, and staff were our anchor, and our church in Salmon Arm continued to be a safe refuge. Pastor Dave was the minister at Broadview then, and made it a point to connect and visit us every time we ended up in the local hospital. Advice time: Be real with the people you can trust, swallow your pride, and graciously accept the support that is offered. It makes all the difference, and you can always repay

the kindnesses back to others when they are in need. What goes around comes around, right?

Hannah's heart continued to grow larger, as her pressures slid upwards. We were familiar or even on a first name basis with most of the paramedics and First Responders surrounding Blind Bay, as they were called to our home so often. I even went so far as to create a medical sheet which listed Hannah's meds, protocols for management, and her specialists' contact numbers at the paramedic team's request to ensure everyone knew how to deal with her before sending out the ambulance. For our family and the neighbours around us, any ambulance siren in the neighbourhood was cause for everyone to run and check Hannah. On June 5th, 2010, Hannah was featured on the BC Children's Hospital telethon, filmed in Vernon at Davidson's Orchard. That was a neat experience for all of us, and seeing the interview on TV reminded us again how dire things must have looked to others.

There is one event that stands out that first half of 2010: I had taken Hannah into our resort pool one summer afternoon, with a crowd of other happy campers enjoying the cool waters on a hot day. Bonnie was in town picking up camp supplies. Hannah was having a great time with a few friends in the water. I was halfway across the pool when she called to me that she needed to rest. She made it to the side, got part-way out, and simply collapsed. I instinctively knew something was wrong when she called, and had managed to force my way across the water in record time to catch her head before it would have hit the concrete pool deck. She writhed for a moment, then went limp. I placed her on a life jacket, yelled for someone to call 911, and began CPR right there, directly in front of a number of families with small children. The ensuing exodus is somewhat funny to reflect upon (it was a virtual stampede to depart the area), but I guess the shock was so hard for many people to see an arrest close up and personal. I later went campsite to campsite to explain what had happened and the positive outcome that had resulted. It was easier to assure the small children than it was the parents, though. Kids astound me sometimes. By the time the First Responders arrived ahead of the ambulance, Hannah was back with us, and we moved her to a more comfortable place in our recreation room. This was the first real crash that many of our guests participated in; I think it was also my first crash alone without Bonnie beside me. With a full house of over 350 resort guests, the story of Hannah gained wings further abroad.

On July 10th of that summer, Hannah had a serious seizure with a resulting low heart rate of under 15bpm that took an hour to stabilize. On August 5th, she had another one we

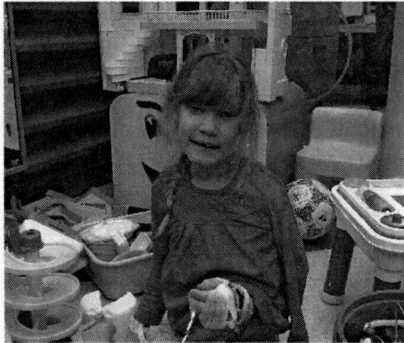

think may have been caused by a bump on her head. We were outside on my Aunt's deck having coffee when Hannah fell off a porch swing. We didn't see it, but we think the swing may have swung back and struck her. She collapsed, went incontinent, and further greyed my Aunt Lorraine's hair. Yet again, our Energizer bunny kept ticking after a bout of CPR. We finished that summer with no other major upsets, thankfully.

7

Deeper into the Valley

THE BC CHILDREN'S HOSPITAL TEAM WOULD OCCASIONALLY fly to an interior city to meet with children and families closer to their home turf. I believe it is a cost-savings measure initiated by the province, and in truth it was convenient. We felt we had a reasonable summer that year (apart from the pool arrest and the seizures), and a confident Bonnie attended a remote clinic in Kamloops at the beginning of September while I was away for the day on business. With an appalling lack of tact, the cardiac specialist whose turn it was to do a rotation completed an echo and then announced Hannah's days were over; that she'd likely die with the next PH event, and that we should prepare to fly to Vancouver for her last days in hospital. Sometimes you have to take the poor bedside manners of some of our healthcare professionals with a grain of salt, but this was a terrible way to drop such news on my wife when she had no support. While Hannah sat on the examination bed, the doctor took his pen and drew out Hannah's heart to show how it would simply explode soon due to the crazy pressure - now exceeding 100 mmHg. Hannah, with her poor hearing, was somewhat oblivious to the doctor, but noticed the tears streaming down her mother's face and asked what the matter was. Bonnie replied she was just missing me, and gathered Hannah up to bring her home. Bon immediately called me from the parking lot to drop the bombshell, and we met back home to absorb this latest bitter pill. All the kids came home right away, and together we tried to pray and comfort one another. Later, as Bon and I hid in our room, our oldest son Joshua came in. He then challenged us to not accept this verdict and to ask for another miracle. He reminded us of where to place our hope. A timely word, but it was with a heavy heart that we awaited the call from BC Children's Hospital to set up the transfer.

School had just started, Hannah was to enter Grade Two, and we were sequestered at home waiting for a call and plane to the coast. We emailed and called our lead cardiologist for news, clarification - anything - and decided while waiting to drive to the area's annual Armstrong IPE fair with family and our close friends from the coast. Terry and Sandy, you are so very important to us! You were with us in Vancouver, you took it upon yourselves to join us when we were crushed, and you have remained close and in prayer for our entire family ever since. What a gift you've been. Hannah was for the most part wheelchair-bound, but could walk some and managed to climb the stairs to a kid's slide with her brother Tim. We snapped pictures, ate junk food, visited the animal barns, and made another surreal memory to take away with us.

Back home, waiting again, we decided to pull together a birthday party for Hannah before we left for Vancouver. I rented a bouncy house, invited the entire Grade Two class, our family, and all friends who were close to us at the time. We had a teary final celebration while pretending for the kids that all was fine. Our adopted camp grandparents, Bob and Ursula, were amongst our guests, and they are another testament to the fine people surrounding us. Bob has since passed away, and our hope is that he saw Jesus in our little girl whom he loved. The party was a heartbreaker for us, but the right thing to do for Hannah. We hosted it at the resort, let the kids swim, bounce, do crafts, and bless our now seven-year-old darling with an outpouring of love.

We set our affairs in order as best we could, and… waited some more. By now, we were climbing the walls, and out of desperation located the direct number of the Edmonton PH cardiologist. Dr. Adatia resides and practices at the Edmonton Stollery Children's Hospital. This man is considered the foremost specialist of pediatric Pulmonary Hypertension in Canada, and much of the treatment options we had tried up to that point came from his research. We called his cell phone, caught him in Europe returning from a PH conference, and gave him a brief update and resulting prognosis. He suggested or agreed (I can't remember which) to see us in Edmonton as soon as we could all be there, and gave us a new lifeline. We called our own lead specialist and requested our file be sent to Dr. Adatia right away as we intended to depart immediately. He agreed, and even if he felt somewhat disrespected by our request, helped us take this important next step. We have the utmost respect and care for this man to this day, who, despite his own personal tragedy at the time, put our daughter's needs front and centre. We keep in touch as often as we can, and know the Vancouver Children's Hospital is better for his expertise and compassion.

Thus began our new relationship with the Alberta health care system, and we can honestly say that both BC and Alberta have fine children's health care regardless of which province you live in. We've had mostly excellent care, despite the odd hiccup, and have learned another nugget of truth: don't attack your health care system, but find a way to work with it. And yes, you do have the power to seek out second opinions within our country's borders, so if you hit a wall at one place, you can and should confirm it elsewhere. Our daughter's life hung in the balance, and there was nothing we wouldn't do for her.

We arrived in Edmonton on the day of Hannah's actual seventh birthday, and checked into a hotel before meeting with Dr. Adatia the next morning. During this night, our oldest son's wife went into labour, and provided us with our sixth grandchild the next day while we were meeting with the doctor. This was another example of how a critical illness can trump life's other important moments; we missed being there for our other children when they needed us too. Looking back, this would be their one spoken disappointment, as their worlds kept turning often without us; we missed some important times with each of

them. However, we don't dwell on it, but make as much effort now as we can to be there for all our kids.

It was September 16th, 2010 when we met with Dr. Adatia and agreed to transfer primary care over to him immediately. Sometimes you just know what's best, and I have Bonnie to thank for her intuitive ability and bulldog tenacity. It's kind of funny - she has sometimes felt second to the tenacity I've had for our business ventures, but in a different way, she's just as tenacious. We make a great team! And I interject here how important it is to have someone close who will walk with you through critical illness, if you are not as fortunate to have a committed spouse with you. You'll need another listening ear when all the medical terms, procedures, and decisions are thrust upon you, and this is not something that should be tackled alone.

Hannah's heart pressures were exceeding the hundred mark by then, and her functionality had dropped to the most critical rating. Yet she did well on a six-minute walk, which made her a most interesting study. Hannah's PH journey is perplexing! Dr. Adatia asked us to trust him with another medication, and spoke of a heart catheterization to be per-formed the following week after admitting her to the cardiac ward. We reluctantly agreed, and left to enjoy a weekend at the West Edmonton Mall before the Monday admittance.

While there, we considered how we could afford the stay in Edmonton and keep Tim with us, and on an off-chance, we called the Ronald McDonald House in Edmonton as a possible source of help. To our relief, we were accepted on an unexpected vacancy, and we moved in that Sunday evening. Friends, an entire new world was opened to us that night and ensuing months, for what started as a few days of consultation turned into a second home away-from-home. We have become so entrenched in the Ronald McDonald family that we consider our time there akin to walking hallowed halls. What goes on within those facilities is miraculous, essential, and life-altering no matter who you are, and regardless of for what reason you've come under their roof. If you can, drop by for a tour, cook a meal with friends, and donate! Nothing can be so rewarding, once you've seen the tragedy and victory that goes on each and every day for the thousands of families they serve.

On Monday, Hannah entered the Stollery Children's Hospital as an in-patient, and we were set up in a shared room on the fourth floor cardiology ward. Different than Vancouver, there are usually two patients per room in Edmonton, with a few single-patient rooms set apart for isolation. We've been banished there a time or two... Unlike Vancouver, only one parent could stay with a child overnight. The Ronald McDonald House became our second home, as it enabled us to keep our family intact. We came with three days worth of clothes, and stayed for three months. Did you know you can get four days out of underwear with just one pair? Right side, backwards, inside right, inside backwards...just kidding. The Stollery Children's Hospital is part of the University of Alberta Hospital, attached to the Mazankowski Heart Institute. There are thousands of patients of all ages, thousands of health care professionals, and thousands of families mixing it up throughout the building; you cannot help but see everything common to man under one roof. It's quite a perspective.

That first day, Dr. Adatia started Hannah on Bosentan, an "endothelin receptor antagonist". This medication helps lower blood pressure in lungs, and is a common treatment for patients with PH. He started Hannah on a quarter of the target dose. This did not go well, and by six a.m. the next morning, she seized and then flat-lined. She recovered before the crash team could begin their work, but she surely scared the bananas out of the entire ward. And thus Hannah introduced herself to the fine people in the Stollery: dainty, delightful, mysterious, and so very fragile. She was moved to ICU, was started at a lower dosage, and has tolerated it ever since. Later that week, she was to have a CT scan, where a simple task of placing an IV was required prior to completing the procedure. Her blood pressure was so low that the nurse couldn't find a vein to access, despite multiple attempts at different sites. Hannah was terrified and hurt, which caused her heart to race to dangerous levels, and finally Bonnie called a halt to the procedure. No one could change her mind, and so back to the ward they went without the IV and scan.

Finally, Hannah was taken in for her second heart catheterization, which she handled much better than the first. Dr. Adatia kept her under for four hours, doing the CT scan at the same time. Interestingly, he kept the cath wires in her while she began to awaken to monitor her heart pressure, and discovered it climbed as she grew more alert. Dr. Adatia came to us with a continued plan of attack, and was confident he could really help her. We had done a lot of praying, and breathed a big sigh of relief as we headed back to the ward.

Hospital life was not bad for us there; they had an excellent team of volunteers working from a central "beach" play area where we spent hours, days, weeks, and months enjoying the programming and security of a well-managed environment. Hannah loves the place still, and Tim will remember specific points with fondness. However, Hannah's pressures were climbing, and were now in the 130 range (they actually hit 178 for a time). At the end of September, a new med was approved for Hannah (who was the first PH pediatric patient in Canada to get it) called Iloprost. It is an inhaled prostacyclin that is taken multiple times a day to open blood vessels. We used a corded vaporizer with saline, which shackled us to a pretty regimented routine. It later came with a nifty chargeable portable box to vaporize it anywhere, freeing us up to travel remotely. For Hannah, this was every two hours, with no help through the night as we tried to balance her need for the prostacyclin with her urgent need for rest. This was an amazing drug, and we could literally watch her heart pressure return to a normal level for about an hour after dosage. This meant that approximately seven times a day she had relief from the pressure within, and we were soon discharged to the nearby Edmonton Ronald McDonald House for the next step in Hannah's care.

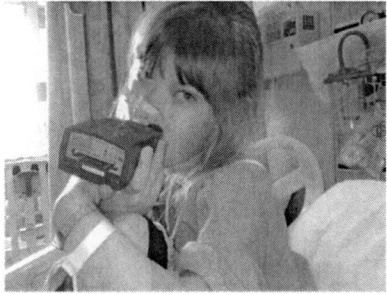

8

A Shelter Found

HERE I TAKE A PAUSE FROM HANNAH TO TALK ABOUT A MOST important part of our journey. In the midst of life down in the dark valley, we had moments of sunshine to help carry us along. Almost as if we had stumbled on a side path that led up a valley wall, we had stumbled into this small niche at the Ronald McDonald House that has changed us significantly as a family. We've lived with people from all over the province (and further) whose children suffer from mild to major health issues - many of whom will live with their health issues the rest of their lives, barring a

miracle. Each House is set up with private rooms for a maximum of four occupants, with a central kitchen to prepare your own foods in. Each family is given a fridge, a freezer, and dry storage shelves, and quite often a group will come in and prepare everyone's meal. In fact, over the years we've been part of the RMH family, we've seen meals increase tenfold and services added such as free shuttling to and from the hospitals. Every city tries to develop their own formulas of success. We've experienced three Houses now in our travels, and appreciate each one. Businesses donate free hockey game tickets, fast food coupons, parking, sometimes products, and we have been humbled with all that has been directed to our family. Hannah collected bagfuls of stuffies, had football and hockey players sign their autographs, and watched Disney characters drop in unexpectedly. Tim was always included. There were bingo nights, movies, special guests, and even an on-site schoolroom with a teacher to help children keep up with their studies. Hannah was seldom able to attend a class, however Tim was a regular and tried to keep up his courses from Salmon Arm with the teacher's assistance. It wasn't really successful, but we appreciated the attempt. Other House benefits: you can do your own wash, sit quietly reading a book, or take the family to the games room to pass quiet evenings. Overall, this setting is very therapeutic.

Tim was much loved at the House as the go-to guy for all things electronic, and the lad to involve the siblings and patient-children in games and activities. He made many friends, briefly getting to know some before they left for home, and sharing in the loss of others who did not make it. He has stood alongside us and dealt with all the challenges a sibling of a chronically-ill child can experience. He entered the House world when he was twelve, and spent part of two school years in a state of flux. One day, son, you will look back and see how important you have been to others, to us, and especially to Hannah. It has cost you something, but in time this will be paid back generously.

We did move around a bit those first three months, for if one of us stayed in-hospital with Hannah while the other ran home to pay bills and see if our dog was alive (smile), we were bumped out of our RMH room for the next family on the list. However, due to the seriousness of our daughter's health, the staff made sure we would be fit back in right away.

On one particular occasion, Bonnie grabbed a flight back to our resort to pay bills, and had a peculiar experience. During the first leg of her journey home from Edmonton to Calgary, she spent her time asking God why suffering occurred. If there are no tears in heaven, how could He explain what Hannah was going through? Instantly, she was 'given' a picture of babies being born. From the child's perspective, nothing good was happening, all was pain and shock, and they simply wanted to go back to where things were warm and comfortable. Then the image flipped to the people outside the womb, who were cheering the baby on to hurry up and get born already. You see, we on the other side know life is wonderful and full of hope and opportunity, and so despite the pain of childbirth, we urge the baby to come join us. Bonnie had a glimpse of Heaven that day, where saints are not grieving for us in as much as they are encouraging us to endure just a little bit longer, as the good stuff awaits through the final door. This earth is not all there is; for Heaven is just beyond the horizon. All that happens here is in preparation for eternity. This was a profound moment for Bonnie, and the vision has become one that we've shared with so many hurting families at the House.

Often the staff would point newcomers toward us, so that we could welcome and encourage them in whatever situation they found themselves. We were by no means the longest-attending family in the House, but we were usually the oldest, and often we could relate as parents to the young couples who came through. We grew to love them so easily, and used our experience as parents of a large family and of parenting Hannah to forge strong mentoring relationships. We were amazed by the speed at which this happened: when faced with crisis for your child, all the worldly trappings fall aside, and no one really cares what you do, what you drive, or how successful you are in business and life. What matters is your kid, your family, and how you will walk through a dark place.

A young couple, Darryl and Kyra, shared our time that fall of 2010, along with their son who was battling cancer. That poor boy endured more pokes, surgeries, drugs, and ordeals than seem fair for an entire lifetime, but he was a source of inspiration and affection to our family and the entire House. As professing Christians, mom and dad lived out an amazing faith, and continue to do so today despite the loss of their only son. Thomas passed away in the fall of 2011, after a long and courageous battle, and it was Tim who suffered the most in our family. He loved that guy perhaps more than we did.

Darryl and Kyra are a couple we keep in contact with, as they find new ways to serve the Lord in their hometown.

Another young lad named Jaxon suffered from another form of cancer, and lost his battle during the same time. I'll never forget the day Jaxon had a new tumour taken out of his hip in the morning, and was asking to play Nintendo DS with Tim by the afternoon. What a trooper, and what a story this family has that could curl your toes. Each of these families is living out the reality of loss in the midst of life, and we think of them as true heroes.

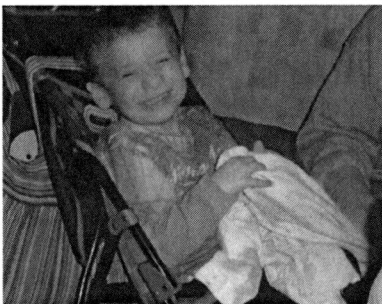

We became quite close to a Mennonite family from central Alberta whose daughter Andrea required a third heart transplant. Her story spanned a lifetime, and we met her when she was a sweet sixteen. Beautiful girl that she was, her stay with us in the Stollery was very difficult as she continued to decline. She was moved off the Children's floor to the Mazankowski Adult Heart Institute next door due to her age, in hopes her next transplant would carry her through into her adult life. We shared meals with her parents Maynard and Faye, and stopped by regularly to see Andrea when she was up to it. Maynard and I would share late night conversations about God, and how His Word fit into our broken worlds. Such fine gentle people - we love this family, and consider them valued lifetime friends. Andrea passed away in late spring 2011 while we were there. One day, we look forward to seeing these children in Heaven, free from suffering as God's Word promises. That will be a glorious day indeed!

For every hard outcome, there were dozens of good. Some friends from our area in BC were transferred to Edmonton Stollery for their daughter's liver transplant. We were with them for some of their Alberta time, until they returned home to enjoy normal life again. Another young lad, Cole, was in the Stollery when we first arrived, and was there another year after. During that time, he endured living with an artificial heart. He couldn't walk or speak, and was essentially a normal pre-teen locked in a virtual prison of pain. We met him very soon upon our arrival, and started letting Tim hang around him whenever we could. They quickly became great friends and could communicate surprisingly well. Part of this was due to Tim's amazing ability to accept others at face value. He wasn't uncomfortable with Cole's disabilities, and involved him in conversation and deed like any other 'normal' child. Cole's smile, his gestures, and his inquisitive eyes spoke volumes to us, and Tim could read him better than most.

One day, Tim and I were at the mall when I thought of the idea to bring some control back to Cole. We found some simple squeeze guns that would fire off a Nerf-like bullet when the handle was pressed. I knew that Cole could use his hands for such as task, so we added the weapon to a rubber squeeze chicken and headed back to the ward. You should have seen his eyes light up when we showed him the gifts! We encouraged him to hide the gun, and then shoot the nurses and especially his artificial heart specialist whenever they tried to poke him. He mastered the idea quickly, and for the first time had some control. And the chicken? Well, after a couple of days and nights of making it scream an unholy death every few minutes, he was asked to retire it to end the nightmares he was causing other children. They wondered what horrors were being committed against Cole behind his 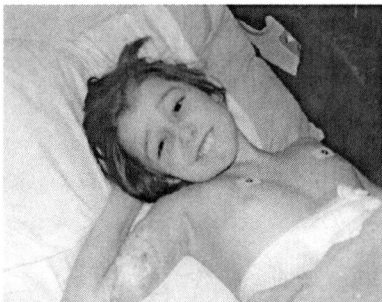 closed door… Such fun, and an important lesson for all: Give your child or dependent control of something in their life! No matter how small, give them something.

I'll interject here to point out that an artificial heart is a last resort for when a person's heart has absolutely no ability to function sufficiently in sustaining life on its own. Hannah was not a 'candidate' for one, as hers worked well despite the pressure mounting within. We were informed that should her heart fail, it would be a catastrophic and unrecoverable event – unlike other cases where a heart would slowly or predictably fail with some measure of warning. In Cole's case, there was time to plan for and insert the device to give him time to strengthen for a heart transplant.

Most of the stories within the Ronald McDonald House end on a positive note, and I quickly realized none of us would be in that place forever. In fact, most were there for a relatively short time, as either their child would get better, or not, or they would outgrow the age constraints of the House. No matter what, the place is only as good as you give and receive, and we committed early on to investing ourselves in others as much as we could. We found that when we were desperate for Hannah, we could find someone who understood, and in fact, we would usually find ourselves encouraged when we saw others in need and responded to them. Therein lies the secret to RMH: there is always someone who has it worse, so if they can do it, so can you.

Incidentally, Cole eventually strengthened sufficiently to handle a heart transplant, and was able to return to Calgary and then to school over the next two years. He's in high school full-time now, and can manage a lot of tasks himself. We became quite close to Cole's parents, and spent many a late night around a kitchen table encouraging one another. Later, Cole made it to our resort and enjoyed a promised tube ride with his brothers. Imagine a highly compromised kid with little control of his limbs, bouncing through waves behind our boat, laughing inside as hard as any teen boy could, living life: a snapshot of joy if I've ever seen one. His family's time ended at the Stollery and RMH, and I suspect he will only return at some point to the Mazankowski Adult Heart Institute for adult care.

Did I mention how much we love the staff and volunteers at RMH? As in any business, the House operates only as well as it is managed, and the Edmonton RMH is blessed with some very talented and compassionate people. It has only improved over time, and we are excited to see where the Director will take things. It has been our privilege to share our story on behalf of the House, and to be an ambassador to the various Ronald McDonald restaurants during the McHappy Day fundraiser. Tim and I were ushered around in a stretch limousine when the new *McCafés* were officially introduced, and have appeared on television a few times. Tim was the star on each occasion, as he had so much authenticity to share from a sibling's perspective. We've been a poster family as medical recipients of the many generous people in our land, and we love to give back wherever we can. There is so much we've experienced at the Ronald McDonald House, so many ways in which our lives were enriched, that it seems a few paragraphs cannot do it justice. Bonnie and I would encourage you again to make a point of visiting the House nearest you, and know you will be touched in a profound way.

9

Finding a New Lifeline

WITH SO MUCH GOOD TO SHARE, WE WERE STILL MIRED IN A lot of difficulty. Hannah's disease was being managed, but at great cost. Our absence from work and home had consequences, and our development was stuck in a mismanaged public process. Funds from our lender grew scarce, payrolls were a challenge, and our strength and energies were at an all-time low. Submitting to our circumstance was not an option - we had no choice. On all fronts, demands, bills, and expectations assailed us. Around us, we watched kids who were afflicted with terrible diseases sometimes have a second and third complication thrust upon them. How could we not question a God who would let such things happen? And so we paced many a miles pouring out our grief and frustration with where we were. Yet, at the same time, we discovered new things daily. While experiencing the tension of wanting out of our circumstance, we counted it a privilege to be there. Can you relate to this? The path lay before us, and step by hesitant step, we continued to walk ahead.

Finally, after several previous attempts to qualify for a BC Provincial health program called the At Home Program, our Edmonton social worker was able to make the case on our behalf that we could no longer return home without physical support. The board of directors who oversee the program met at Donna's request, and unanimously approved our application for nursing support despite Hannah's ability to accomplish tasks that most other applicants could not. Because of our nursing need, we were then accepted for the overarching At Home Program. It was a back door route to the same end. We could finally return home with the promise of a new safety net for Hannah.

We were discharged from Edmonton in mid-December, and returned home to enjoy Christmas with our family. Bonnie met with program coordinator Katie in late December 2010 for a preliminary meeting. You cannot imagine our gratitude for the At Home Program and Nursing Support, after dealing with so much of Hannah's care on our own. Now with five years of the program under our belt, we have all seen the direct correlation between home care and Hannah's recovery. She is a shining success for British Columbia to take pride in! Interestingly, Hannah arrested on our deck an hour after that first meeting when she stooped to pick up her cat off the outside deck. Bonnie was alone for this one again with the collapse occurring as I was on the phone with her. There I was, speeding home from almost an hour away, with no word of the outcome until I was almost there. Stressful times.

As an aside, our daughter Rebecca consorted with our local newspaper during late Fall, and on December 3rd, before we were able to return home, an article was ran that invited the readership into our daughter's life. We were made privy to this just before it came to print, and we struggled with allowing a community that had opposed our development so vehemently to know our most personal struggles. Pride. It's a hard thing to swallow, isn't it? A direct outcome of the article was the establishment of a trust fund that enabled us to purchase essential hospital-grade monitoring equipment we could not have possibly returned home without. And it led to an eventual thawing of many of the hardened hearts against us, most of whom had opposed us without understanding our plans and goals. May we never have to experience this again in our lifetimes! But in hindsight, it was okay and has led to better relationships with a number of people around us.

The At Home Program immediately gave us access to supplies needed for Hannah's medications, relief from the actual med costs, and most importantly: nurse support in our home and at school. This has proven to be perhaps the most significant point in our journey, as we were no longer alone in our fight for Hannah, and could share the burden of vigilance with others trained to intervene as needed. A team of nurses were selected for us, who began to share night monitoring for several nights per week. This meant that Bonnie and I could try to sleep without the worry that no

one was watching our girl, and for the first time in almost two years we could attempt to relax a bit. Bonnie remembers the freedom of going to the bathroom without the monitor in tow, of all things! The program also meant Hannah would have a nurse present during school hours, to ensure she had the best care possible while trying to live as normal a life as possible. The school opened their doors for the extra care, and I'm sure it made for some interesting challenges for the class and teachers as all adjusted to another person in the room. Hannah now had an Education Assistant and a nurse for the days she was able to attend school.

We too had to adjust. There have been a few awkward times with all the traffic in our home (I can't walk around half-naked at night, for example), and we have a lot of fun memories. Memories of things said, cabbages flushed, floods, devices melted, running into Hannah's room in underwear to do CPR together, tears spilled, and small and large victories. When you are in the trenches with people for the sake of a life, you tend to discard the fluff and experience relationships in powerful ways. The younger nurses have become like daughters, while Lona is more like a sister to us. They've seen us at our worst, and I'd like to think at our best, and yet we still are fast friends. Not bad, eh? As Katie reminds us, this isn't always the case for some families. The environment at home is not conducive to long-term relationships for a variety of reasons, so there is a constant parade of gals in and out. If you ever find yourself in such a place, do what is necessary to provide a safe, warm, and caring home with sufficient privacy for all to ensure you keep the right help. The nurses are entering a unique working environment which they are not typically trained for, and it takes a concerted effort to make it work.

I've joked how fun it would be to take the lot of them through the pharmacy checkout with the stash of vividly labeled Viagra boxes we used to pick up. Shoppers and tellers could not look me in the eye when I'd plop down ten boxes of the stuff at a time, standing there with a Cheshire cat grin. At that time, the media was caught up in unfolding polygamy events near Creston, BC, so it was easy to draw the connection. Comical moments…

I did put one of our nurses, Val, through a particularly harrowing event one night later on in our journey. Our cardiac specialist had written me an email advising that Hannah was not having true cardiac arrests, but rather brief periods of syncope that would resolve themselves if we let them play out. I was quite offended at the time, and remember stewing on this for a bit until Hannah's next cardiac event. It was somewhere after two a.m. one early morning when Val called out to us to come running. Hannah had fallen off the cliff again and become totally unresponsive. The monitor showed no heartbeat, no respirations, and so I assumed the lead in performing CPR. Bonnie was at Hannah's head with high-flow oxygen and a finger on her neck pulse, while Val took position on Hannah's femoral artery in her leg. I began reciting the "I, I, I, I, staying alive, staying alive" chant, changing the words to time with compressions. "Imagine our doctor telling me this isn't an arrest." I then commanded Val to record what would happen next, to be that 'professional' opinion that we weren't, and stopped CPR entirely. During the compressions, the girls would register a pulse to time with my pushes that instantly stopped when I stopped. I remember angrily telling Val to then record the change with CPR, and began again. Of course, they both felt the pulse, upon which I threw my hands up again to stop it a second time. Val was quite upset with me then, and told me to quit fooling around. Hannah recovered after I resumed, and we combined Val's written record with the tear strip taken from the monitor to deliver to our cardiologist. The trace proved the pacemaker was firing, but our experience proved the heart wasn't filling. I was not certain I'd proven my point to everyone's satisfaction, but it felt good to me! Listen, if you are ever near me when you suffer a heart attack, be sure there's nothing you need to prove, or I just might on your behalf! You'll feel good about it later... honest!

Lona shared recently how impacted she was upon her first home visit with us. The level of anxiety and stress prevalent in our home overwhelmed her, and she says she could not believe how we had survived life to that point without assistance. She remembers too, how we'd try to allow Hannah to experience normal things in the course of her life. After one serious PH event in the middle of the night, I asked Lona to bundle up and join us as I took Hannah snowmobiling around the resort the very next morning. Perhaps we would be questioned at times for the things we did, but we believe it is imperative to let go where we can, and to allow Hannah to

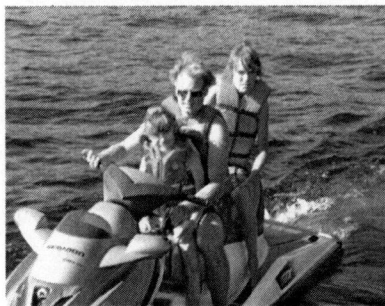

'risk' things a bit despite her condition. We'd recommend to any caregiver to give thought to this, as all of us long to be normal, if even for a few moments. We concluded, when things were at the very worst, that Hannah still needed to live, and to experience the thrill of living where she could. And so she did (and does), carefully, but intentionally. Where a concerned parent may see risk, a child sees opportunity and adventure, and Hannah was no different. She would often ask us to try new things, and did not see her disability as an obstacle to many new activities. Hannah has climbed the wires at Sky Trek, east of Sicamous; ridden the West Edmonton mid-sized rollercoaster; made it halfway up the Freedom of The Seas cruise ship climbing wall; and even managed to ski for the first time with oxygen. She can't exert herself long, but we let her try what she feels up to (with parameters). It never fails; every time we are in Edmonton, Hannah wants to go to West Edmonton Mall to either visit the amusement park, or swim in the fantastic waterpark they have. We never tell the ride operators what Hannah suffers with, as all attractions are clearly posted to prohibit people like her from attempting them. If they ask why she is in a wheelchair, we then opt for truth and have never been turned away so far. Remember Cole, and the tube ride we gave him? He would be the first to approve of our stand on this.

In addition to our fine At Home team, we have worked with numerous nurses who attended Hannah during her frequent hospital stays. Sometimes our contact would be brief, other relationships continue to this day. In as much as we are fumbling our way through this disease at times, our nurses too have had to approach Hannah somewhat differently. Hannah responds to a gentle touch, and submits to often painful procedures with an amazing gentleness and trust that usually draws her nurses right in. Many of these nurses are the age of our eldest daughter, some are older, and all have their own lives and stories that influence them. Breaking past the professional barrier is a goal of ours, and we've established some real friendships as a result. One such nurse is Jessica, from the Edmonton Stollery, who poured out a genuine love for Hannah that won her the favourite nurse of Edmonton award. Most often our interactions with nurses have been excellent. The odd exception has not come about intentionally, but rather through a moment of carelessness such as the one young nurse who came a hair's breath away from mixing up two very incompatible meds. Had we not been there to catch it, the outcome could have been catastrophic for Hannah. Our specialist reminded us it is our job to be vigilant for Hannah. We have every right to question and oversee our daughter's care, and virtually every nurse we've met has appreciated our attentiveness. I cannot stress this enough: nurses have lives too, and they are not perfect. We cut them some slack and ask for the same in return.

⚞ 10 ⚟

A Moment of Sunshine

WHILE IN THE EDMONTON STOLLERY THAT FALL OF 2010, we had been approached by the Make-a-Wish Foundation and were encouraged to take advantage of a generous gift to grant a Wish trip for Hannah. Her recovery was not abrupt, or even really strong, but was sufficient that we were eventually released to go back home in mid-December. We enjoyed a family Christmas back home, with Hannah wheelchair-bound and on oxygen twenty-four hours a day. In January we returned to the Stollery for a checkup which confirmed that Hannah's pressures were climbing once more. We decided we should act on the gracious offer of a family trip to Disney World. This new focus gave Hannah a much needed boost, and the Foundation began to send us details and the itinerary of the week-long adventure. It is worth mentioning that a single family was behind our Wish trip, hailing from North Vancouver, BC. We were able to make contact and share emails, phone calls, and photos with two very fine people who gave from their heart. I recall asking them why they supported the Make-a-Wish charity, and their response was perhaps reflective of many others who support it; they felt they had been blessed in life, and wanted to bless someone else in a tangible way. Should you ever read this story, friends, I hope you realize how important this trip was to Hannah's future, and to our emotional well-being!

Our trip took place on March 2-10, 2011, with Bonnie, me, and our two youngest children bundled off on our way in the loving care of this organization. Looking back, I suppose we could have had a nurse accompany us, but I believe it never occurred to us to ask the At Home program. We did on a later trip, but here, when she was most vulnerable, we were used to doing things on our own and proceeded accordingly.

From the minute we departed our home to the moment of our return, all expenses were covered, all theme park passes supplied, all medical equipment provided, and we were met at every step of the journey by kind people. Our destination was the Give Kids the World (GKTW) resort, located outside Orlando, Florida. The airline crew and passengers applauded

Hannah as a Make-a-Wish recipient, and both kids were invited inside the cockpit during flight despite the U.S. 911 security protocols. We were met at each leg of the journey

and escorted through airport securities. Once in Florida, we were given keys to a new Dodge Caravan for the week, and directed to a half-duplex in the heart of the GKTW village. You can see this amazing facility online at gktw.org to better imagine our delight and amazement. The resort is run by staff and volunteers who ensure the visiting child and recipient family are catered to in all ways. In one fairytale-like building, there are over 106,000 stars adhered to every visible portion of the interior lofted ceiling, each inscribed with a child's name and visit date. GKTW, started by its founder Henri Landworth in 1986, has made the dreams of close to a half million people come true, giving families the opportunity to experience life memories despite the frailty of their children. And we are now counted alongside so many others who have benefited from Mr. Landworth's vision. Hannah has her star located alongside the tens of thousands before her, plus a commemorative paver stone, and we've been able to return since to see them both forming part of the collage of stories.

Hannah was much weakened at this point, and spent much of the time sleeping despite the wonder of the village, theme parks, and rides. She was unable to participate in most of the many rides available, but still counts this trip as a highlight in her young life. Tim and I had V.I.P. passes, and tackled any and all challenges at will. We tamed every rollercoaster, and were always escorted to the front of every line as a Make-a-Wish family. At nights, we'd all eat ice cream and pizza, throwing out every carefully-followed diet regime we had in place for Hannah. There is one ride that stands out to Bonnie and I: The Kali River Ride. What a joy it was to see Hannah's eyes sparkle as she got soaked and jostled with the rest of us! Hannah enjoyed this ride twice, giving her the thrills of water, rapids, and drops in a lush tropical setting. She also went on the Jurassic Park ride, and a Pterodactyl hang-glider that perhaps she shouldn't have, but wanted to regardless. We all were startled when the T-Rex came charging out of the dark on

the Jurassic park ride, and were glad we could not see Hannah's heart rate at that moment. We might have had heart failure ourselves! We were intentionally allowing Hannah to do what she felt up to, and we follow that same intent to this day.

We returned home, thinking we may have had the one and only major trip with Hannah we'd get, despite our efforts to retain hope and fight the odds. It brought us back to the drive we had made to the Armstrong Fair the year before, when we had been told she had only days or weeks to live. The GKTW village was a daily reminder of how tenuous her hold on life was, and knowing a high percentage of Wish recipients lost their fights to live, we went around in a sort of fog. Neither of our kids clued into the reality of the GKTW statistics, although we were able to share this with them much later. It was a lot for us to take in, but as we were struggling in some ways, it may have been this trip that really woke Hannah up to want more. She came away from that experience more prepared to fight, a drive that was so needed as we turned the next corner.

11

Over the Cliff Again

THINGS WENT FAIRLY SMOOTHLY FOR THE NEXT MONTH, until the evening of April 17th, 2011. My parents and sister were visiting when Hannah suffered the first of a string of cardiac arrests. My family had never seen an event, and I remember how shook up they were to experience the crisis firsthand. We remained home through the night, deciding to exchange a run into the local Salmon Arm hospital for an early morning drive back to the Edmonton Stollery. We made it as far as Jasper National Park, five kilometres inside the west gate, when Hannah awoke from a nap, looked funny, and crashed. As quickly as I could, I pulled over beside Clairevoix Creek so that we could place Hannah onto firm ground for CPR. This event stands out head and shoulders as her worst crisis with just us present: Bonnie did CPR while I scrambled for the oxygen tank and tried to stop traffic for help. One burly guy in a Dodge truck saw me waving the O2 tank, stomped on the gas, and slewed around me on the ice and snow. I suppose I looked like a deranged threat instead of a desperate father? Big chicken! Fortunately, an elderly couple in a truck and camper saw us and pulled over. Miraculously, they had a two-way radio on board that the Jasper RCMP just 'happened' to monitor in that moment. While the RCMP raced towards us from town twenty minutes away, Bonnie performed CPR on the snowy road. Meanwhile, I lay beside Hannah administering oxygen and looking for signs of recovery. I clearly recall a bit of life coming into her eyes after about ten minutes, like a lamp undimmed, but it faded and we lost her again for another five to ten minutes. All the while, Bonnie was calling out to the Lord to save Hannah, to give her back, and to rescue us from harm. I looked into my girl's eyes and saw the emptiness of life without her, and had no words to utter to God. Time stopped, traffic was halted, and only when the RCMP officer arrived did Hannah start her slow and agonizing climb back to us. What I haven't repeated is that for most of her cardiac arrests, Hannah would often start screaming an unholy scream before collapsing, and would usually scream her way back to us as her cardiovascular system 'reset'. This must be what heart attack victims feel, so perhaps they can identify with our girl. I feel sorry for the crowd who gathered to witness her event, for they no doubt will remember the horror of pain Hannah must have endured this day among so many others.

It didn't take long after she came around for the ambulance to arrive, and once stabilized, she was given a lift to the Jasper hospital. She was fussed over and surrounded by incredibly attentive staff who lined up an airlift to the Stollery with our specialist. What was amazing to all was Hannah's rapid recovery in the hour or so we were there, to the point where she had nurses and doctors laughing with her. She was (and is) so endearing… We completed that leg of our journey by air ambulance, returning to our second home in search of answers. Somewhere through this period, we met with a neurologist named Dr. Sinclair. He took a keen interest in Hannah and began to study her for seizure activity. Several times he captured proof of frontal lobe seizures that he believed were the root cause of her arrests, and asked to start her on anti-seizure meds. We agreed, and began to introduce her to the first. We had quite a scare the first day or two, as she hallucinated and acted hostile and emotional, but as promised, she settled down quickly, and has never had any negative effects since. We believe Dr. Sinclair made an important diagnosis, and attribute part of her recovery to his work today.

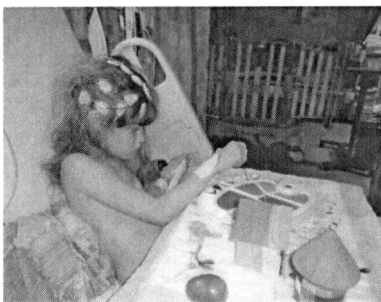

Once again, Hannah stabilized enough so that we were able to return home for the Easter long weekend with a Holter device. Dr. Adatia had previously tried to catch an entire episode on monitor, and decided she could escape the hospital while wearing the portable device. So back home we went, just in time to participate in a scheduled Easter service where our family was the focus. Pastor Dave invited us to share our story in full, and to describe what it meant to trust God when so much was going wrong. Bonnie shared that no matter the outcome, God IS good, and has a plan that is unfolding. More so, she shared our belief that healing doesn't last forever on earth, but in Heaven. For Hannah, we were asking for His healing touch day-by-day, and thanking Him for each moment we had with her. We encouraged others that they too could trust God no matter what, and ended the service on a high note. Recently, my son John found the service posted on YouTube, so if you are interested you can meet us there, at https://www.youtube.com/results?search_query=baskill+family. Or you can just type in Baskill Family in the search window of YouTube.com. And yes, that is our son John jumping out of an airplane just below the Easter service video. Hmm, I wonder if Hannah would like to try that?

We enjoyed a family gathering that afternoon with all our kids on a perfect spring day in the Shuswap. The very next morning, however, Hannah stepped out the front door with Tim, and crashed. On the front deck of our home, we administered CPR again, to which Hannah responded favourably. While the First Responders awaited an ambulance, I took the Holter to our phone and transmitted the tail end of the cardiac arrest to our specialist and cardiac team. That got the wheels churning! Just before she was loaded into the ambulance, Hannah, with tears in her eyes, asked to see her pet snake before she left. Tim had caught one for her earlier that we had placed in a cage, so, without fanfare, we allowed her to handle the deadly viper (not) while several of the paramedics retreated to a safe distance. One First Responder who happens to supply our resort with flowers each year was especially squeamish, and we tease her about it still. What young girl loves to handle snakes, and where did I go wrong?

Shortly after we arrived in Salmon Arm, a BC Medevac Services helicopter was on route to us in town to ferry us to Kamloops Airport for transfer to a rapid-response Medevac jet. That was an amazing ride for me, although Hannah was quite out of it for most of the journey. The jet was a converted Israeli fighter jet, capable of carrying eight people at a cruising speed of 850 km/h; it delivered us in record time to Edmonton in just over thirty-five minutes. Bonnie drove out ten hours behind us with Tim that same day, April 25th. I love to drive, but I'm sure glad I was the parent chosen for those flights!

Over the next few days, we agreed to allow the pacemaker installation, and were scheduled for surgery as soon as a room became available. One hospital crisis after another kept us from our date until May 4th. At the same time, a new medicine called Remodulin was ordered for Hannah to be administered via subcutaneous deliv-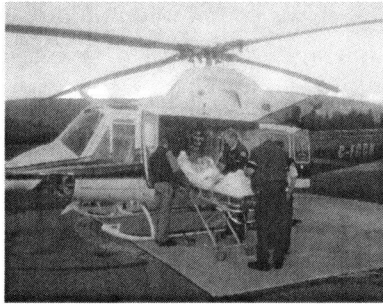ery. This would begin a few days following her surgery. Hannah tolerated the initial surgery well, but became fevered and worsened in ICU immediately after. Once Hannah seemed stabilized Bonnie had left to pay bills back home, but she did not make it an hour out of town before Dr. Adatia discovered that Hannah's pericardial sac was filled and compressing her heart. She was rushed back into the OR for emergency surgery to place drains, which scared the pants off of us. By the time Bonnie returned, Hannah was in the procedure. That was a hard thing for me to do by myself: sign papers and release our girl back for a second surgery in crisis without my Bonnie to help shoulder the decision. I can only imagine how it must feel to be a single caregiver making such choices.

God really is good, as our daughter survived and made a slow recovery afterwards. Make no mistake: we respect and acknowledge the skill of our cardiologist, and would not want to minimize his part in this. However, we submit to a higher authority whom we believe has the days of our lives numbered. And again, He gave us more time. On May 10th, Hannah was moved from ICU after successfully starting the sub-Q Remodulin. So much was happening at this time: the Slave Lake fire started, Tim and I were RMH Ambassadors to the McHappy Day Edmonton event, our dear friends lost their only girl, and Hannah crashed again and again. Despite the pacemaker, her cardiac events and arrests continued at the Ronald McDonald House on May 13th, then again on the 14th, then on the 16th just after our friends' daughter's funeral. We were in and out of the ICU and RMH like a yo-yo, until discharge May 19th. On May 20th, Hannah had another arrest at breakfast at the House, with numerous families gathered around, and we refused to be taken back in. The responding paramedics stayed with us until early afternoon, after which we bundled up and left directly for home. We literally snuck out of town, against the expressed counsel of the paramedics and Stollery team. We were so exhausted and so

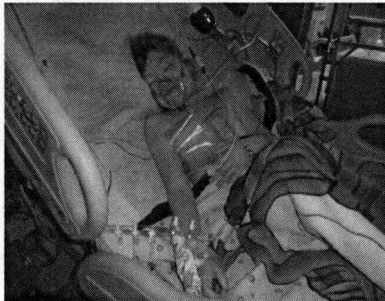

overcome with the continued unrelenting pace of disaster that we felt it best to return our daughter to her own home, bed, and cat. That was Hannah's desire: to see her cat Chaz (by then the snake was forgotten). We had perhaps resigned ourselves to making her last days as comfortable as we could, away from the sterile environment of the ward and ICU, where nothing more could be done. It was a sobering drive back through the mountains into the wee hours of the morning…

❧ 12 ❧

Bottom Dwelling

OVER THE COURSE OF THE NEXT WEEK, SEVERAL FRIENDS and family members made their rounds to encourage us, and perhaps to see Hannah one more time. She was so weak, carried everywhere, on oxygen full-time, and weighed under forty pounds. Her muscles had wasted away, but she maintained a positive attitude despite it all. Hannah would ask us often about heaven, and sometimes she would wonder why she was unlike other kids her age. She noticed, and in her simple way she mourned. Bonnie was so good at sitting with her in bed, sharing stories from the Bible, and giving her insight into how deep God's love is for each of us. She would remind Hannah that heaven is where we will all be free from suffering, and where we will meet all those who have gone on before. One day Bonnie was given another cool picture in her mind of Hannah entering Heaven's gate, seeing all the wondrous things ahead of her, then turning back to see her parents coming in directly behind despite an interval of time here on earth. She wouldn't be alone and need not fear. Bonnie also pictured the departure from this world to Heaven like the shedding of an old jacket to place on a new one. Not so scary when you look at it from another viewpoint... much like the image she had earlier of the birth of a newborn. Hannah would take great comfort in these talks and I would be amazed at how the Lord was meeting my wife. She was much encouraged too by these visions.

We would lay her outside on a mattress on warm afternoons, move her ever so carefully, and maintain our close vigilance. Our nurses were back in full force, and we were so desperate for any respite. On May 27th, Hannah arrested overnight. June 10th brought another arrest of over four minutes. June 11th brought us again to two events, spread apart by less than four hours. On the 12th, she again arrested at four p.m. The next arrest came on June 19th, followed by one on June 25th. We were living pretty much minute-by-minute instead of day-to-day. While experiencing a caffeine overload, have you ever felt like you couldn't catch your breath? Nerves,

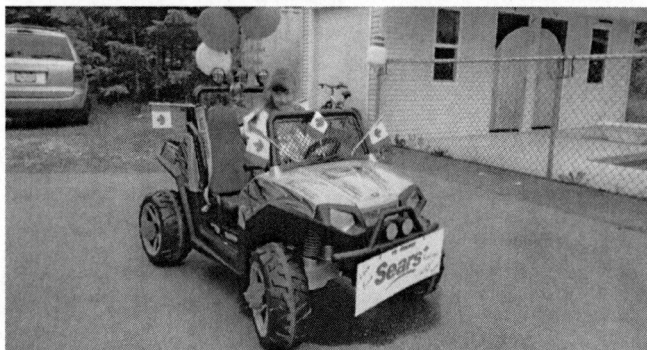

stress, lack of sleep, ongoing work demands, the parade of well-meaning folk coming by to offer condolences, tip-toeing around others for lack of knowing what to say... that was our life on the basement floor at the bottom of the valley.

My older sister, Sherry, took it upon herself to do something nice for Hannah. She spoke with the Kamloops Sears Canada in mid-June, and together they arranged to bring a cool battery-operated riding car all the way from eastern Canada to our home in time for our annual Canada Day parade and celebration. Here in Blind Bay, we have a party that starts at nine a.m. with the parade, features kids' games and activities and music at a nearby park, then concludes with fireworks at the end of the day. Hannah was invited to attend the parade riding in the car that had been delivered the very night before, and you can imagine her excitement. The staff from Sears Kamloops met with Sherry, her husband, and my folks to present the gift and to wish her well on the eve of Canada Day. She went to bed with anticipation, and awoke to another gripping cardiac arrest at eight a.m. on July 1st. I was assembling our resort float when Bonnie called in a panic, and without a word and with many onlookers I jumped in my truck and tore away from our café and up our incline to the house. The lumber I carried was thrown across the main road. Our staff dutifully picked it all up and finished the float, knowing something terrible had happened once again. After she clawed her way back, she fell asleep, waking forty-five minutes later in distress that she might miss her ride. How she pleaded with us to let her into the parade! So we made the snap decision to load her monitor and oxygen, and together with her nephew, she drove ahead of us through the entire parade while we marched behind with everything needed to run to her defense. Of the several thousand people crowded along the route, perhaps only a few realized the triumph of her ride, and how perilous her life was in balance. For us, we knew all too well, and chalked it up to another snapshot that God was giving us to remember her by. Hannah was invited with Tim to raise the flag at the park field by the parade marshal who knew of her plight. Although we had felt sorely treated by many in our community because of our development, there were many who encouraged us, prayed for us, or offered the empathy of a grieving heart for such a lovely young girl in distress. Thank you, Blind Bay!

~13~

Tremors and Earthquakes

JULY 4ᵀᴴ BROUGHT A HARD ARREST THAT HAD HANNAH screaming her way in and back out for a long time after. We went into the local hospital for monitoring, but refused to return to Edmonton. On July 8th, 2011, Hannah recorded her thirtieth official (our count) cardiac arrest, requiring CPR for over two minutes at three in the morning. Some of her arrests were preceded by evident seizures, which confirmed the treatment plan of our neurologist, but not all. Our records show events occurring on the 17th, 18th, and 20th. And just as consistently as the cardiac events came, she screamed going in, and for minutes afterwards coming out. The sound is seared so well into our minds that we can pick it up from far away. In fact, I can't recall exactly how many times Bonnie has woke up and arrived at Hannah's side before she even began to scream.

She just knew, and would often wake up believing God had prompted her. I equate it to the incident in our resort pool, where I just knew and was on my way to help before she had evidenced her need.

Our cardiologist had implored us to return to care in Edmonton, and 'coincidentally', we started getting messages and calls from a few of our key cardiac ward nurses who were also encouraging our return. Jessica, shown here, is one of Hannah's favourites, who Facebooked us several times wondering if we'd come back. I'm sure they all must have felt for us, and wanted to be the support we needed as we awaited the end. There was talk of drilling a hole into her skull to perform some sort of pressure test, but we were steadfast in our decision: Hannah would remain at home where she was most happy.

Our oldest daughter and son-in-law had attended a small Pentecostal church in Salmon Arm while briefly living there, and they encouraged us to seek out the prayers of an elderly couple named Bill and Janine if we could. We called, and agreed to bring Hannah to Living Waters Church that next Sunday. We arrived after the morning service, the four of us together with Bonnie's older sister Kathy and her grandson who were visiting at the time. Kathy, as a cardiology nurse from the U.S., had been our go-to person to understand all the technical terms and procedures we had tried, and had recently driven from Oregon, Washington a week or so earlier to be with us. We were so glad she was with us, and could be a part of what happened next.

It is important to note that hundreds and thousands of people have prayed for our daughter through the most difficult times, and we had a social media Facebook page following that numbered over five hundred friends. Our church family prayed, our closest friends prayed, we prayed, and even those who confess no God prayed. We knew God had heard us time and again, and was continually giving us miracle after miracle for all to see, yet we were desperate for something more. We wanted there to be a lasting healing for Hannah, otherwise we implored Him to simply end her suffering if things worsened. We didn't arrive at this point easily. We held our faith intact, but were so weary and spent. Something had to happen.

And so on this memorable day, these saints gathered around us to hear our story in greater detail. Then they did a surprising thing: they turned to Hannah, and asked her what she would ask for if Jesus were there in this room beside her. They clarified the question, focusing on Hannah's one single most important wish she would ask Jesus to grant that day. Hannah, with no prompting, shared her desire for her "heart seizures" to stop. Hannah was just shy of eight, had endured crisis after crisis, had seen some children die while others got up and went home, and was dependent on others for virtually everything in her life. She could have asked for anything, but she zeroed in on this one desire. The good people of Living Waters listened, went apart for a short while, and then returned in agreement to pray for exactly this one wish.

We learned something monumental in our faith journey there: God is very, very interested in the smallest details of our lives, and desires for us to be honest and forthright with our closest fears and wishes. We have learned to be way more specific in our prayers, for on this particular day, in the midst of all that was going on in the world around us, God reached out of Heaven and gave our girl the very desire of her heart. For after that day, she has never once suffered another arrest, period. They stopped. Suddenly and surely, and to this day over five years later, she has been seizure and arrest-free.

To be fair, these same people prayed for our sister Kathy, who departed for home only to discover she was in a stage four battle with cancer that she lost only three months later. We don't understand why God chooses some, and not others, but He is God, not us. Perhaps one day we will find our answers in Heaven. Perhaps these answers will make sense.

⚜ 14 ⚜

The Long Climb Out

WE NOTICED IT ALMOST RIGHT AWAY. ONE DAY SHE WAS weak and defenseless; the next she had spunk and drive. It seemed that the very next day Hannah was asking to stand, and to venture away from her wheelchair. She rallied daily, and by the end of summer could walk some distances by herself and was more engaged in activities around her. We returned to the Edmonton Stollery for follow-up clinics, and were advised her heart pressures were above 150mm Hg. It made no sense, but she seemed to be strengthening as her pressures worsened to an alarming level.

We didn't make it back for the starting day of school, but a few days later made an appearance as class was underway. Hannah walked down the hall, shed her coat and put on her inside shoes, then opened the door and entered the classroom.

Her entire Grade Two class turned in shock, and then burst into tears and shouts as they rushed to surround her. Everything stopped: her teacher, the E.A., our nurse, and I stood aside and watched an entire group of angels love on our girl. To this day, I have never experienced anything like it, and I can't think about it without choking up and marveling at the very presence of God in children. These were the same kids who had started with her in kindergarten, who had written cards and stories for her while in the hospital, and who had prayed for her every start of class and often at home. Parents have come to us to tell how Hannah has impacted their child, and we again are reminded of the good that happens in the midst of bad.

Our life began to turn towards normalcy. We gained confidence in Hannah's stability, and began to take a date night out here and there. We could shop away from home, and even spend a night away while nurses cared for Hannah. And we could re-enter our business. We had not realized how hard we had worked to juggle everything until we began having time to focus individually on our work roles. Tim and I did some long-delayed fishing and outdoor activities, with Hannah able to attend more often than not. It didn't happen all at once but rather over the course of couple of years to the point where we can say we live a fairly normal and healthy life.

Apart from our recovery (for it truly was all of ours to experience), life around us continued to have its ups and downs. As mentioned, we lost sister Kathy in early December, Bonnie's sister-in-law had a diabetic reaction after a simple knee surgery and died abruptly the same week, and I lost my mother only three weeks later to an unexpected respiratory failure. We lost three members of our family in three weeks, and knew we weren't exempt from the reality of life, despite Hannah's improvements. Kathy chose not to try conventional chemo and radiation, and Bon was able to spend a week with her before she died. One day my mom was looking forward to Christmas with us, and the next day she was in respiratory failure that led to further complications. I was the one who broke the news to her that she would not recover, and helped make the decision to end her care a week before Christmas. Bonnie and I struggled many times with our losses, and grieved not being able to phone Kathy or Mom to share Hannah's recovery and milestones. We still grieve this today, but temper our sadness with the knowledge that we'll see them again in a far better place.

15

Equipped for the Task

HANNAH CONTINUED TO IMPROVE, AND AS SHE BECAME more comfortable with the subcutaneous medication and needle insertion, we believe the Remodulin was starting to have its intended effect. Hannah's pressures peaked at 178 mm Hg in late November 2011, and then began a slow but steady decline that has continued to this day. Her six-minute walks began to improve, and her need for assistance in routine activities lessened. And she grew! She gained weight, and has grown to a normal percentile with her peers. Children with De George Syndrome do not normally achieve normal heights or display good growth curves, so in this she is an anomaly. And children with PH do not normally bottom out and recover as stellar as she has. Again, she is a study, this girl of ours.

Remodulin has proven to be an exceptional drug for her, which she has tolerated well with virtually no side effects. It provides continuous twenty-four hour support - unlike the inhaled Iloprost. We wonder about the future with Remodulin, as one day it seemed that the effectiveness of Iloprost just quit. Will Hannah quit responding one day to Remodulin as well? Time will tell, but we know there are several dose increments ahead that give us a comfort zone as she matures. And we look forward to the day an oral version, which is in clinical trial, will be effective for Hannah. She would love that!

We have offered our experience to anyone considering the subcutaneous Remodulin to treat aggressive Pulmonary Hypertension. We've learned a lot about site care including what symptoms to watch for, how frequently a site change should occur, and how to maximize freedom while wearing the pump. We've tried different body locations and needles, settling on her upper arms as the best spot with a Silhouette needle so that the pump can be worn on the same arm with a length of Tubi-Grip.

This really works, and Hannah has a custom-made dry-suit arm band for showers and swimming. This is so important to her, and we encourage all to try it. I personally do most of the site changes and care, and have things down to a precise method. I know for the most part what to look out for, as do our nurses, and we've surely saved Hannah from some infections or unnecessary site changes as a result. And yet we were hesitant to make the change to

Remodulin at first! Perhaps some of you reading this book may find helpful insight that will dispel some of the mystery of the disease and its treatment, and we welcome your emails and calls should you need further support from an experienced family.

We also began a herbal treatment in 2012, set up by an amazing man in Kelowna who is passionate about natural herbal treatments. We ensured there would be no interference with Hannah's prescribed meds with our specialist and pharmacist, and began a parallel treatment that continued right up until this last year. John's intent was to help support Hannah's major organs against harmful side effects common to the medications she is taking, and argue as you might, Hannah has made a most unusual recovery. Her liver function is excellent, her digestive system is healthy, her resistance to infections and viruses is normal, if not elevated, and… she lives! Don't forget that part: Hannah has overcome all obstacles and is prospering. Bonnie is always researching and looking for possible causes, and our own Dr. Adatia has encouraged us to keep on doing whatever we are doing. And so we shall.

$\sim$ 16 $\sim$

Higher and Higher

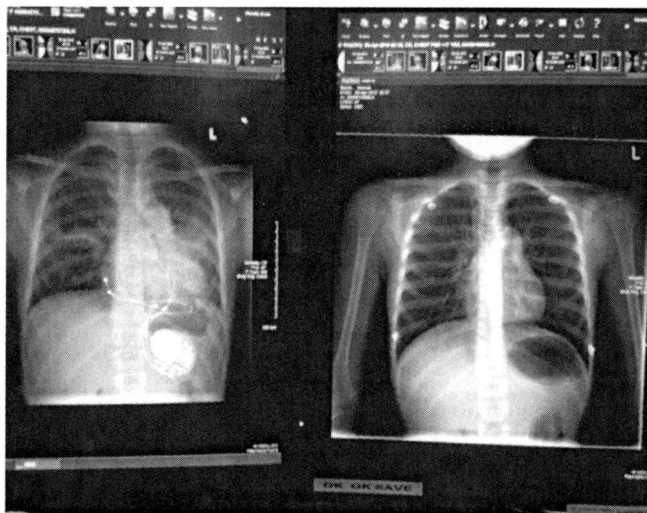

IN SEPTEMBER OF 2012 WE HAD A SETBACK WHERE HANNAH contracted pneumonia and was hospitalized for close to a week in Vernon, BC. Bonnie reminds me it was here that Hannah asked why she had to go back to the hospital (she was quite sick and emotional), and I suggested it may be to share with someone there that Jesus loves them. A couple of days later, she asked her attending nurse if she knew Jesus, and told her He loved her. The young woman was deeply touched, and had to take a few minutes to regain her composure. We may never know how our words affect others, but perhaps these words of Hannah's were delivered innocently at just the right time to one who needed to hear them.

I remember the day we drove in to Emergency for the pneumonia. The on-call resident physician took an x-ray, compared it to one from a year or two before, and called me over to look at it. He was in disbelief, for her heart was filling half of her chest cavity, leaving little room for lungs and organs. He thought he was breaking horrific news to me, man to man, to protect my wife and child. We've seen him several times since, and have a great rapport with the entire Salmon Arm Emergency team. I now keep photos of both x-rays on my phone, and have looked at them periodically to remind me of her journey. I now need to add a third, which shows a more-appropriately sized heart in her chest cavity, comparable to more normal kids of her size and age. Anyhow, Hannah bounced back, and returned home without further complications.

That same year, Hannah was recommended to run the torch for the Rick Hansen Relay for Life that occurred in October 2012. Hannah was now in Grade Three, still supported by oxygen and a wheelchair for longer trips, but able to walk her portion of the Salmon Arm run directly alongside the entire King's Christian School, who had assembled to cheer her on. That was another memorable day which we were honoured to share with others. So many other worthy recipients ran with the torch, and the final assembly at the City Hall was a testament to many incredible people. Speaking of King's Christian School, we never detected anything other than love and respect for her from this fine student body and staff, and count it our privilege to have walked the most difficult part of our journey with them. Hannah no longer attends there, as she is now home-schooled to catch up on a lot of missed studies, but they remain dear to us.

In 2013, we were able to book an extensive vacation accompanied by our nurse Lona and her son. We took a cruise first, and finished with a few days back at Disney World. It was on this trip that we were able to return to Give Kids the World, and Hannah was able to see her star and paver stone while standing unassisted. She was much stronger, and appreciative of the splen-
dours around her, and we were humbled to be able to come back intact as a family. Lona was able to share in this time with her son Zak, and to be a part of our journey with us as over-comers.

In late 2014, we were able to complete a public rezoning of our resort lands. We attribute a portion of our success to the breakthrough Hannah made for us in the community. It's difficult to paint a picture of how our business goals were hampered by a community, by Hannah's disease, and by our own attitudes without detracting from the main story, but I can assure you they were. Looking back, it is easier to see now that

there was a divine plan in everything that happened, even if the outcome wasn't exactly what we had planned for ourselves. Had things gone really smoothly, and had our business made us the kind of money we envisioned at the start, perhaps we'd be less the people we are today, having brought harmful influences to our children or even our future business decisions. I am certain we would have been less compassionate or aware of the needs of others, and would have missed meeting some very wonderful people. Plus, we would not have this story to pass to our children and grandchildren that is as much a part of their heritage as it is our reality. As mentioned earlier in this book, our lenders too have been an integral part of this, and even if the shareholders behind them were reluctantly dragged along, they allowed us the freedom to attend to our daughter first. The very fact that we stumbled across this land and were able to acquire it for our ambitious plans is another testament to the forward-thinking of our Lord. For it was the equity in this land that really provided the financial means for us to be sustained thus far, and I suppose our hoped-for "profits" were taken early in the form of wages when we just weren't present and on duty. So, to look at the bright side, much has been gained instead of dwelling on what we might have lost. And we trust God to enable us to complete and honour the debts we've accrued during this time.

This year, in the spring of 2015, we reluctantly accepted a second Wish trip, this one organized by the Children's Wish Foundation that had been offered to us over five years prior from our time in the Vancouver Children's Hospital. The wonderful staff of this non-profit group had written to us over the years, and finally called in late 2014 to encourage us to take a 'celebration' trip with them. They had all of Hannah's records and they knew we had taken a Make-a-Wish trip, but they told us that funds had been set aside for the past years awaiting our decision to act. So we agreed, and let Hannah pick a Wish that took us to a Mexican beachside resort for a week. There, she snorkeled with her dad and brother, lay in the sun, caught small fish and crabs, dressed up for dinners, and took in the beauty of the ocean fully aware and engaged. We were humbled by the gift, and see now how important the celebration idea was for all of us. It marked a true return to life, and propelled us further along our road to recovery.

We've seen tremendous change and maturity in Hannah, and look forward to the day she returns to graduate with her former classmates. In the meantime, we are enjoying working with two nurses who provide daytime care for Hannah, and who have stepped into our home school program with enthusiasm. Nadine and Lona both share responsibilities through the week as together we manage her health, and they are deeply loved by Hannah. Our one remaining night nurse Sothea gives us a couple of nights a week to sleep well, as we still monitor Hannah to this day. I think this is a crucial truth: compromised children (and adults too, I'm sure), need consistency and a whole health approach to nurse care. We are so grateful to the BC At Home program that supports Hannah so well, and we know the program can take much credit for the successful outcomes for Tim, Bonnie, and I as well. It is said that over 80% of marriages fail under the weight of a chronically-ill child. We have experienced some of the crip-

pling stress that could break a family apart. However, the At Home program with its nursing and pharmaceutical support, our friends, and our faith in God have made our outcome favourable, and we can take our experience to others to help them win the same result.

Tim is now seventeen in grade twelve, and he enjoys an abundant and full life with friends and family. He's caught more fish in our lake than anyone I know, and he hunts, motorbikes, hikes, and works at various jobs when he can get them. Hannah is in Grade Seven, and has made leaps and bounds in her catch-up schedule. She participates in theatre, dance, and song classes, and is intent on learning violin. She is

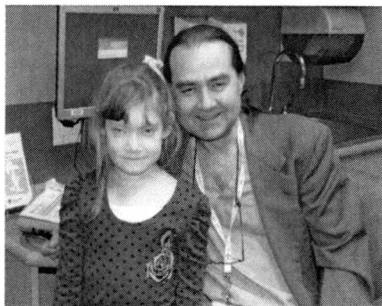

almost as tall as her mother, as tall as her oldest sister, has long blonde beautiful hair, and smiles and laughs every day. She submits to my dastardly poking during site changes with aplomb, and encourages children wherever we go to find joy. She's not shy about her experience, and is honest and believable when she talks about it. We get excited thinking of the possibilities she has in making this world a better place, just because of her story. And we share it with anyone who wishes or needs to hear it because of something they are enduring. In fact, we most often follow what was modeled to us: we ask what specific wish or desire you might ask of the Lord, were He to appear right beside you to grant one thing. And no, He likely won't give you a new Lamborghini! Nice try, though…

17

Arriving at the Summit

TO OUR KNOWLEDGE, THERE HAS NOT BEEN ANOTHER PH survivor with such a tale, but that could be because others have simply not survived the first arrest (or we have incomplete Intel!). So much more work needs to be done, both in genetic studies and treatment options, and we long for the day when this disease is not only managed better, but is eradicated. Hannah's journey is being documented for further study, and our beloved Dr. Adatia is a world-renowned leader in the fight for a cure. You'd like this man. He is soft-spoken with a curious pony tail and open-back clogs, and he is married to another prominent cardiologist that has herself made an indelible mark upon this world. How they manage their work and a family of teenage girls is beyond me, but do we applaud their commitment! For where would we be today without them?

We truly appreciate all the cardiologists, our neurologist, resident doctors, nurses, lab and administrative staff, and others we will never meet who are behind Hannah's success. And we look forward with hope and confidence for the future she will have in the years to come with their continued support. Her story has left a lasting impression upon everyone she has touched, and we'd like to think we too have left our mark. It's certainly true for us: all these fine people have impacted us profoundly, and helped us see life around us more fully.

We talk about Hannah's experience a lot around our house. Sometimes we'll see Hannah do something new that we'd thought she'd never accomplish, or we'll catch her in a moment laughing like any other pre-teen. And we'll wonder: what caused this disease? Why has it manifested itself so unusually in Hannah? Why has she experienced such a remarkable recovery where others have not? How did she not suffer oxygen deprivation during at least one arrest, and why is it that she had immediate care at every one of her known crashes? Is it fate, chance, or plain old good luck? Or is it something more… Could there be a divine plan? From the outset of this book, you know this is our belief: our journey through the valley didn't happen by accident. We've encountered a number of parents who grieve their own losses, and have heard their broken cries asking why their children had to die while others (our daughter for one) have gone on to recover and live. There are no pat answers of course. But once again, God gave Bonnie a verse that helps us with the bigger picture that we now share with others. Isaiah 57:1 says "Good people pass away; the godly often die before their time. But no one seems to care or wonder why. No one seems to understand that God is protecting them from the evil to come."

I suppose it all comes back to perspective. We may see a child's life lost as the worst possible tragedy, and point our fingers at a God who would allow such a waste while criminals seem to get away scot-free. God reminds us He sees all things, and in His great compassion He saves many from the harm that is yet to come. We look at eighty years as a good measure of life; God looks at eternity. Would we not rather our kids spend forever in the presence of our Creator, instead of possibly risking that future by demanding a full measures of days here on Earth? The Bible says that God knows our days and numbers them. I believe we can trust Him whether our days be short or plentiful. Bonnie and I claimed this verse for our own when we knew Hannah was on the razor's edge. And we've shared it with our friends who have lost their beloved little ones when they sincerely wanted an explanation they could hang onto. For what else can we offer? How else can it make sense?

I am reminded of a dialogue I had with a man who attended a dinner at our resort a few years ago. We were in the midst of our valley, home for a bit, and our talk shifted to this man's grandson who had died following a short lifetime of living with Cystic Fibrosis. He shared how his thirteen-year-old grandchild came to visit him three weeks before he succumbed to the disease. He awoke one night to hear his grandson wheezing and struggling for air during a frequent attack, and rushed in to see if he could help. The lad shook his head, and his grandfather sat there with no words to offer. Upon sharing this, he looked at me, and with sincerity told me there is no God, and that although he was glad I found solace in a meaningless crutch, it was simple genetics that played an impersonal game of Russian roulette. He himself had been given a sturdy body for seventy-plus years, while his grandson had not. And that was all he could offer his dying grandson - nothing but a kind presence. Absolutely not a shred of hope.

In the absence of hope, there is death, and were it possible for me to roll back the clock, I'd sit at that boy's side and tell him about a wonderful God who would make all things right in perfect time. I am so sorry for what this man now takes to his grave, but I am relieved for the Word of God promises that all children will be ushered into His presence until they are old enough to choose for themselves. I will see this child again in perfect health.

We closed our conversation that night with my giving him an illustration. Suppose he was right, and there was no God. We live; we die; and we end up in a coffin feeding worms. Seems pointless, but there you have it. Live well today, for tomorrow you... end. I think I'd steal that Lamborghini if I couldn't afford it; after all, what would I really have to lose? I'd better grab all I can before I disappeared like a puff of smoke, right?

On the other hand, what if my faith proves true, and there is a God: one who extends the free offer of grace and life eternal, but who also stands in judgment of those who reject Him? Now we don't end up with our carcasses feeding worms, but stand before two gates - one leading to life eternal with God the father where I'll be heading with surety, and the other leading to eternal separation from all that is good. Christians call this Hell and equate it with fire and brimstone, but I see Scriptures defining it as forever separated from the family of God. No love, for God is Love; darkness only, for

God is Light; and incredibly alone, for God is our Friend. God says He loves us so much that He will respect our right to choose, and He will honour it for all eternity. If we reject Him, we still experience His love, for it's His love that would hold Him to respect our choice. Does this make sense? Lee Strobel presents this view in his powerful book *The Case for Faith*. All seekers should read this, really.

Either way, there is much at stake in this scenario. On my friend's account, we cease to exist; on the other (a fifty/fifty bet in the world's eyes), we will stand before our Creator. I, as a believer, have nothing to lose and everything to gain, while my friend has *everything* to lose and nothing to gain. And he buys lottery tickets to 'win' his financial freedom for his remaining years through a one in twenty-seven million chance. That's his idea of a good gamble…

Returning to Hannah, I'm a logical person who likes to touch, feel, and understand the world around me. I look for tangible evidence to prove or disprove the things that perplex me, and have found nothing either medically or statistically that can solely explain her journey. There is the evidence of a miraculous hand underneath it all, that although we were not spared the hard stuff at the bottom of the valley, we have been able to overcome and rejoice - if even for the moment. Wounded, yes, scarred… for sure. But we are standing upright, facing our future with confidence that our God cares and has a plan for our lives that culminates in a perfect hereafter as promised in the Bible. We have learned, above all, to cling to the promises He has given us. A favourite verse that has carried me is Jeremiah 29:11: "[11] For I know the plans I have for you," declares the Lord, "plans to prosper you and not to harm you, plans to give you hope and a future." This verse has been with us for much of our married lives, but was never so meaningful as when we were at our lowest looking upwards for hope.

Once in a while a verse or passage comes along that is a real nugget. Again, Bonnie discovered it (you'd think I never read, wouldn't you?) Our entire experience can be summed up with one very amazing passage, found in 2 Corinthians 1:8-11: "[8] We do not want you to be uninformed, brothers and sisters,[a] about the troubles we experienced in the province of Asia [Alberta]. We were under great pressure, far beyond our ability to endure, so that we despaired of life itself. [9] Indeed, we felt we had received the sentence of death. But this happened that we might not rely on ourselves but on God, who raises the dead. [10] He has delivered us from such a deadly peril, and he will deliver us again. On him we have set our hope that he will continue to deliver us, [11] as you help us by your prayers. Then many will give thanks on our behalf for the gracious favor granted us in answer to the prayers of many." Friends, we have life: Hannah has been delivered, and the prayers of many have been answered. We are so thankful!

I spoke at the outset of finding a purpose in the valleys of life: our purpose may be to help families endure and overcome. By sharing our experiences with others at the Ronald McDonald House, at the hospital, and with people we encounter to this day, we've helped others gain a new perspective. It hasn't been all that bad for us, and I'd like to think no matter the troubles that come our way, there will always be some good. Bonnie has another verse that has meant a lot to us, found in Romans 8:28: "[28] And we know that all things work together for good to them that love God, to them who are the called according to his purpose." In living it - walking it out - we become more genuine and empathetic people. Isn't that a worthy goal? To be a help to others based on our experiences, to make life more sweet and purposeful? Bonnie would leave you with this thought, as her heart's cry for each one of you.

You are only in the valley for a time, or a season, and we encourage you to make the most of it. Lofty viewpoints give way to storm clouds, paths lead over unexpected edges, and sometimes we find ourselves way down in a deep valley, leaning on others to help us find our way back. But as much as we need people around us, none can come close to the reality of God in our lives who has not spared us the bottom. Down there, we found life and purpose. And He didn't leave us there. We overcame. You can too. The valley will be put behind you.

I'm going to end our story here. Thank you for reading, and for seeing our heart. It's not about us, but about a God who loves us and has a better plan. We have a purpose, and for our faith, we will live forever in a far better place. Our journey is not over with Hannah, and it will certainly be epic! This book relates a real love story from the God who created and loves our daughter to her family, to her home nurses, and to the many health care professionals who have poured out their hearts for her. We'll enjoy the views from up top once again. We know that another trip down through the valley is approaching one day, where we will continue to fight the good fight. Friends, enjoy the moment,

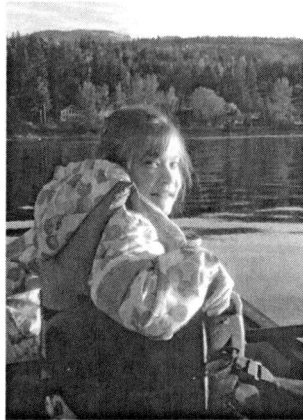

embrace life, and seek the one true God who will make it all worthwhile.

Dan Baskill

For Bonnie, Hannah, and Tim Baskill

Dan Baskill Bio

DAN BASKILL IS A HUSBAND, DAD, GRANDFATHER, ELECTRI-
cal contractor, and resort land developer. Residing in beautiful Blind Bay on the banks of the Shuswap Lake, British
Columbia, Dan is co-owner and manager of Blind Bay Resort
with his wife of thirty-two years, Bonnie.

Together they have six children, four of whom are grown
and married and who have given
them ten wonderful grandchildren
so far. *Through the Valley*, which is
his first published book, chronicles
a celebration of successfully navigat-
ing the challenges of life through
perseverance and an abiding faith.

CPSIA information can be obtained
at www.ICGtesting.com
Printed in the USA
LVOW07s0456031216
515623LV00001B/4/P

9 781773 020136